TWAYNE'S WORLD AUTHORS SERIES

A Survey of the World's Literature

INDIA

Mohan Lal Sharma,
Slippery Rock State College
EDITOR

Munshi Prem Chand

TWAS 488

Munshi Prem Chand

MUNSHI PREM CHAND

By GOVIND NARAIN

Acadia University

TWAYNE PUBLISHERS

A DIVISION OF G. K. HALL & CO., BOSTON

First Printing

Library of Congress Cataloging in Publication Data

Govind Narain, 1927 -
Munshi Prem Chand.

(Twayne's world authors series; TWAS 488 : India)
Bibliography
Includes index.
1. Srivastava, Dhanpat Rai, 1880 - 1936—Criticism and interpretation.
PK2098.S7Z597 891'.43'36 77-28454
ISBN 0-8057 6329-5

MANUFACTURED IN THE UNITED STATES OF AMERICA

For the late RAJ KUMAR KOHLI,
scholar, gentleman, and friend

Contents

About the Author

A native of Jaipur (Rajasthan), Govind Narain completed most of his schooling in India as well—having received his B.A. and M.A. degrees from Agra University and the University of Rajasthan respectively. After teaching English at Delhi University for a number of years, he went to the University of Toronto as a Commonwealth Scholar and took his Ph.D. degree there. Since that time, he has taught at Delhi University and Acadia University in Canada.

Govind Narain has been associated with the Indian Association of English Studies, the Association of the Canadian University Teachers of English, the Modern Language Association of America and the Northeast Victorian Studies Association. His publications include an edition of Dryden's *Essay on Dramatic Poesie* as well as articles in *The Indian Journal of English Studies, The Dalhousie Review, The International Fiction Review*, and *African Literature Today*. Presently, he is working on book-length studies of Samuel Butler and the Indian-English Novel (1930 - 1977).

Preface

Prem Chand has received a great deal of critical attention since his death. Only a few of the books published are, however, critical in a real sense. A large number were originally written as M.A. and Ph.D. dissertations. They present a mass of evidence to substantiate the writer's thesis but usually shy away from analysis and comment. Of the others, even the best confine themselves to a discussion of his political and social ideas, basing it on the axiomatic truth that he was a "progressive" thinker. There is very little attempt to unravel the different strands in his personality and thought. The novels are generally taken either as case histories or as social documents and are hardly ever considered as works of art in their own right.

Prem Chand was keenly interested in the social and political questions of his time and it is not possible to do justice to his work without viewing it in its social context. But it would be a mistake to reduce it to its sociological constituents. Its significance is larger and deeper because it deals with the perennial issues of life. Prem Chand's heroes, in their existential quest, are looking for some kind of order and coherence which can give meaning to life. In spite of his involvement with contemporary affairs and trends of thought, the concept of this meaning is derived from the age-old Indian tradition. And the quest for meaning makes Prem Chand not merely an artist but also a moralist and "sage" in John Holloway's sense of the term (see *The Victorian Sage: Studies in Argument*, London, 1953).

While pointing out the limitations of the purely sociological approach, I have tried to ensure that the political and social import of his work is not neglected. But, in keeping with my emphasis on him as a moralist and sage, I have attempted to bring out its cultural and moral significance. The first three chapters are devoted to an examination of his general philosophical position, viewed in relation to the traditions both of the East and the West. The main stress in the rest of the study is on a close analysis of the individual novels, respecting their integrity and autonomy as works of art. Bearing in mind the needs of the Western reader who may not be intimately acquainted with them, I have furnished plot summaries of the novels before taking them up for critical consideration. The short stories have, owing to limitations of space, received only a brief notice.

Every student of Prem Chand owes a deep debt to Mr. Amrit Rāi and Mr. Madan Gopāl for their untiring labors in making available, besides the novels and short stories, the letters and essays of the author. I have great pleasure in recording to both these gentlemen my sincere gratitude for permitting me to quote from the above. Since no separate bibliography of Prem Chand's writings is available, I have relied on Mr. Madan Gopāl for details of first publication of the novels and on Mr. Amrit Rāi for those of the stories. I am also grateful to Mr. Jainéndra Kumār for permission to quote from his book on Prem Chand, and to Mr. Goyankā for permission to reproduce the outline of the unpublished novel and extracts from Prem Chand's letter to the Raja of Śitāmau.

I express my sincere thanks to Mr. Iain Bates of Acadia University Library for his valuable help in preparing the index. No words can express my sense of appreciation for Chancellor Sylvia E. Bowman, the General Editor, and Dr. Mohan Lāl Sharmā, Editor of the Indian Section, for their infinite patience.

GOVIND NARAIN

Acadia University

Chronology

1880 Born at Lamhī near Benaras on July 31, the only son of Munshī Ajāib Lāl and Anandī Devī; given the name Dhanpat Rāi but called "Nawāb" by the family.

1888 Mother dies; father marries again.

1896 Dhanpat Rāi is married.

1897 Death of father; burden of supporting the family falls on Dhanpat Rāi's shoulders.

1898 Passes the matriculation examination with second-class marks.

1899 Becomes teacher in Mission School, Chunār.

1900 Joins government service as teacher in school at Bahrāich; transferred to Pratāpgarh after about two months.

1902 Enters Government Training School in Allahabad for two-year teacher training course.

1903 Begins writing in Urdu journals in one of which first novel *Asrār-é-Mābid* is serialized.

1904 Appointed teacher in Pratāpgarh school on completion of training; transferred to Kanpur.

1905 - 1909 Stay in Kanpur where he meets Dayā Narāin Nigam and starts writing for *Zamānā*. Marries Shivrānī Devī in 1906 though first wife is still alive. Publishes *Premā* and *Kishnā* in 1907 and *Soz-é-Vatan* in 1908.

1909 Begins five-year stay in Hamīrpur District as subdeputy inspector of schools.

1910 Reprimanded by district officer for short-story collection which is confiscated; adopts pen name "Prem Chand."

1912 *Jalvā-é-Isār* (Urdu version of *Vardān*).

1915 *Prem Pachīsī* I, collection of 25 stories in Urdu.

1916 Passes intermediate examination; son Shripat Rāi born (daughter Kamlā born in 1913).

1917 *Sapt-Saroj* and *Nav-Nidhi*—short stories.

1918 *Sevā-Sadan* (Hindi version of *Bāzār-é-Husn*).

1919 Passes B.A. examination; Urdu *Prem Pachīsī* II and *Prem Purnimā*. Birth of second son who dies next year.

1920 *Vardān* and Urdu *Prem Batīsī.*
1921 Resigns government service; accepts headmastership of Mārwārī High School in Kanpur; son Amrit Rāi born.
1922 *Premāshram;* resigns job in Mārwārī School and joins Kāshī Vidyāpeeth in Benaras.
1923 Establishes Saraswatī Press; *Sangrām,* a play, Hindi *Prem Pachīsī* and *Prem Prasoon;* also *Ahankār,* Hindi translation of Anatole France's *Thais.*
1924 *Karbalā,* a play; accepts job in Gangā Pustak Mālā in Lucknow owing to losses in the press.
1925 *Rangabhumi* and *Āzād Kathā* I; *Nirmalā* serialized in *Chānd.* Comes back to Benaras for the next two years.
1926 *Kāyākalp* and *Āzād Kathā* II.
1927 Begins five-year stay in Lucknow, where he accepts editorship of *Mādhurī; Pratigyā* serialized in *Chānd;* nominated to membership of Hindusthānī Academy.
1928 Sued for libel for his story *Moté Rāmjī Shāstrī;* collections of stories in Urdu, and Urdu version of *Rangabhumi.*
1929 *Nirmalā* and *Pratigyā* in book form.
1930 Starts his own magazine *Hans;* wife Shivrānī serves two-month prison term; meets Jainéndra Kumār.
1931 Gives up editorship of *Mādhurī; Ghaban* published.
1932 *Karmabhumi;* assumes responsibility for *Jāgaran,* a weekly.
1933 Attends Hindi Sāhitya Sammélan in Delhi.
1934 Losses in *Hans* and *Jāgaran* oblige him to join film company in Bombay.
1935 *Jāgaran* closed, *Hans* handed over to Bhārtīya Hindi Parishad; tours South India; enjoys the tour and is pleased with reception; leaves film company and returns to Benaras; *Mānsarovar* I.
1936 Visits Delhi, Lucknow, Lahore, and Nagpur; *Godān;* dies October 8.

CHAPTER 1

Life

THE year 1910 was important in Prem Chand's life. The collection of his short stories, *Soz-é-Vatan* (Anguish of the Nation), published two years earlier, had attracted the attention of the authorities. He was summoned by the district officer, an Englishman, and asked whether he was the author of the collection. He admitted that he was. The officer, after wanting to know the purport of each story, told him in an angry tone: "Your stories are full of sedition. Thank your stars that you are under British rule. Had the Mughals been in power, both your hands would have been cut off. Your stories are biased, you have defamed British rule."[1] The final verdict was that he surrender to the government unsold copies of *Soz-é-Vatan* and not publish anything in the future without the approval of the district officer. So far Prem Chand used to write under his nickname of Nawāb Rāi (his real name was Dhanpat Rāi, but his uncle used to call him fondly Nawāb Rāi—"Prince"). To get around the prohibition imposed by the authorities, Nawāb Rāi now started writing under the pen name of Prem Chand, which was suggested by his friend Dayā Narāin Nigam.[2]

This brush with authority, which obliged Prem Chand to adopt a pseudonym, was not a solitary affair. His entire adult life was passed during the period when India was engaged in its epic struggle for freedom from the powerful and pervasive British Empire—the *Raj*—and the search for its own identity and self-respect on which its right to nationhood and freedom would be based. Prem Chand's life was touched by the freedom movement at every point and it was never away from his thoughts. He was born and lived in Uttar Pradesh (the Northern Province), the heart of the famed Āryāvarta (The Land of the Āryas), which had been the center of Indian civilization both in the time of the ancient Hindu empires and of the later Muslim ones. The British had first made Calcutta their capital, but they could not resist the temptation of moving to the imperial city of Delhi, which was more centrally located than Calcutta. Though the cultural renaissance in modern India had started in Bengal, both Calcutta and Bombay became active centers of the movement for political freedom. But soon, owing to a variety of circumstances, Uttar Pradesh became the hub of the movement. Prem Chand took a keen interest in the activities of the Indian National Congress, adored Gandhi, and had great respect for the Nehrus. In 1921, responding to Gandhi's call for noncooperation with the alien government, he resigned his position in government service and henceforth assumed a more open role in the freedom struggle. He regarded himself not as a leader but as a modest soldier in the battle for the nation's freedom, the soldier whose weapon was the pen.[3] Prem Chand's first short story, written in 1907, was entitled "The Most Priceless Object in the World," the priceless object being nothing else than "that last drop of blood which is shed in defence of the nation."[4] The set of values implicit in this assessment remained with him to the end of his life.

Prem Chand in this respect is not so much unique as typical—typical of the educated and awakened Indian who was in search of his lost soul. Political subjection seemed to him the greatest hurdle in this search, but he was aware of the other hurdles too. He knew, for instance, that this subjection was not the cause of his being lost; more likely, it was its consequence. He was therefore more inclined to blame himself, his own society, his own country, rather than any foreign power, for his miserable condition. Freedom, before being won, had to be deserved. And once the Indians made themselves deserving of this freedom, no power on earth would be able to withhold it from them. Prem Chand's espousal of the cause of India's freedom is therefore singularly free from chauvinism or irrational hatred of the British whom he, in fact, admired in many ways. His critical gaze is directed at his own countrymen who, in their purblind folly, had made themselves slaves of ignorance and superstition and brought down a once glorious civilization to the lowest point of wretchedness and degradation. In all these respects, Prem Chand's work represents the main movement of the Indian mind in the first three and a half decades of the twentieth century.

Prem Chand was born on 31 July 1880 in a small village called Lamhī, about five miles from the holy city of Benaras. He came from a rather poor family, middle-class no doubt but, because of its poverty and lack of status, at the lowest rung of the middle-class ladder. His father was a petty clerk in the post office. His mother died when he was only eight and the father married again. The stepmother was illiterate, unkind, and stingy, and Prem Chand's life became miserable. She was totally lacking in culture or refinement, and Prem Chand's references to her are not very complimentary. The only childhood companion was a young cousin who lived in the same house as Prem Chand himself and went to the same teacher.

His earliest schooling was in Urdu and Persian, the instruction being provided by a Muslim teacher whose chief occupation was as a tailor but who coached some pupils too. Prem Chand started going to him when he was eight and continued for about three-to-four years. He draws a fascinating picture of his life during this period in his short story "Theft":

With my cousin Haldhar I used to go for tuition to a Maulavi Sāhib (Muslim scholar) in another village. I was eight. Haldhar (he is now in heaven) was two years older. Every morning we used to leave after a breakfast of cold bread, taking a snack of peas and barley for lunch. Then the whole day was ours. There was no attendance register at Maulavi Sāhib's nor was there any fine for absence. What was there to be afraid of then? Sometimes we would watch the parade of the sentries in front of the Police Station, sometimes we would pass the whole day following a showman who dances monkeys or bears, sometimes we would go out in the direction of the railway station and would watch trains. We had more knowledge of the train-timings than perhaps the Time-Table itself. . . . Sometimes we absented ourselves for weeks, but we would invent excuses which immediately mollified the Maulavi Sāhib. Had I that much imagination today, I would write a novel which would astonish everybody. Now the situation is that I can think of a story only after a great deal of straining of the mind. Anyway, our Maulavi Sāhib was a tailor; he taught pupils as a pastime. We two cousins spoke very highly about Maulavi Sāhib to the peasants and potters of our village; in other words we were traveling salesmen for our Maulavi Sāhib. We felt greatly elated when he got some work as a result of our efforts. On days when we could not think of any good excuse, we would take some present for Maulavi Sāhib—half a *seer* [about a pound] of peas sometimes, about half a dozen canes of sugar, or green ears of wheat or barley. The Maulavi Sāhib's anger would subside as soon as he saw these presents. When these things were not in season, we would think out another way of escaping punishment. Maulavi Sāhib was fond of birds. There were different kinds of birds in cages in the school. Whether or not we got the lessons, the birds certainly did. They also used to learn with us. We would show great enthusiasm in preparing gram flour for these birds. The Maulavi Sāhib used to ask the boys to get hold of butterflies because the birds were particularly fond of them. Sometimes these butterflies used to serve as scapegoats for us; by sacrificing them we used to turn Maulavi Sāhib's angry moods into pleasant ones. (*Mānsarovar,* V, 111 - 12)

Some other chores were also done—getting fresh green leaves for the goat, bringing groceries from the market, and the typical chore for the eastern pupil, preparing the teacher's hubble-bubble.

This is not an untypical picture of a village lad's education in Northern India in Prem Chand's time and even much later. Government schools had not yet reached the villages. The instruction was in the three R's but the main emphasis was on Persian. As soon as the pupils had learned the alphabet, memorized the declensions, and acquired a steady hand, they were introduced to the classics of Persian literature like the works of Sā'di. The method of instruction was primitive and unenlightened, mostly by rote, with no attempt being made to explain the linguistic, historical, or critical issues. And yet, judged by the results, it was not a bad, unsuccessful, or harmful system. It laid solid foundations on which one could later build as high as one wished. Some of the products were even outstanding, for instance Prem Chand himself. He naturally chose Persian as one of his optional subjects until he received his B.A., but this was not all. Prem Chand did not simply read or write Persian: he admired and enjoyed the Persian classics and they deeply influenced his cultural, philosophical, and moral attitudes.

His father's job was transferred, but Prem Chand stayed in Lamhī so that his studies might not be disturbed. There was nobody to look after him, and he soon learned things which are better left unlearned at an early age. He started smoking and was not careful about the company he kept. Later he moved with his father to Gorakhpur and was admitted to a regular school, first Rāwat Pāthshālā, where he started learning English, and then the Mission School. Nawāb was more or less on his own and here he became absorbed in reading oriental tales—Maulānā Faizi's *Tilism-é-Hoshrubā* (Astonishing Magic), a work of fifty thousand pages, which he began at the age of thirteen and finished in two to three years, and the tales of Mirzā Rusvā and Ratan Nāth "Sarshār." The list also included G. W. M. Reynolds' *Mysteries of the Court of London* (8 volumes, 1849 - 56) in Urdu translation. After the tales he took up the *Purānās* (sacred texts of Hinduism), also in Urdu translation.

Nawāb studied at the Mission School in Gorakhpur up to eighth grade. To pursue his studies further he moved to Benaras, where he entered Queen's College. It was a hard life, and Nawāb walked to the school five miles from his home in Lamhī everyday. He was now fifteen and his father was already negotiating for his marriage. The marriage was duly solemnized, but it was a grevious disappointment. The bride was ugly, almost illiterate, and ill-tempered. He had to appear for the matriculation examination the following year, but his father died and the examination was taken a year later in 1898. He passed in the second division, which made it extremely difficult for him to seek admission to college. But the urge for education was very keen, so he moved to the city and started coaching the son of a lawyer. In the plenty of spare time available he continued his reading in fiction—Pandit Ratan Nāth Dar's *Story of Āzād*, Devaki Nandan Khatri's *Chandrakāntā's Offspring*, and also Urdu translations of the novels of the great Bengali novelist Bankim Chandra Chattopādhāya.

Through a stroke of luck he got a teacher's position in a small Mission School in Chunār, a small town about forty miles from Benaras. The salary was eighteen rupees a month which "at that time was above the highest flight of my dispirited fancy."[5] On this salary he had to support his wife, his stepmother, his half-brother, his stepmother's younger brother, and himself. Once, after a visit to his native village Lamhī, he needed money to cover travel expenses for the return journey. There was no money available. Nawāb came to Benaras and, for two rupees, sold his woolen jacket which, after great difficulty, he had bought only a year before. The job in the school was terminated because Nawāb Rāi's behavior was thought to be too independent.

Once again back in Benaras, he started looking out for a job and got one as an assistant master in a government school at Bahrāich on a salary of twenty rupees a month. But after only two and a half months he was transferred to Pratāpgarh. From here he was sent by the school to obtain teacher training at Allahabad where the principal, Mr. J. C. Kempster, was very pleased with him. This training lasted two years. Immediately after his return to Pratāpgarh, the principal recalled him as headmaster of the Model School attached to the Training College. From here he was transferred to the Government School in Kanpur. The same year, 1904, he also passed the Special Vernacular Examination of Allahabad University in Hindi and Urdu.

In Kanpur Prem Chand met Munshī Dayā Narāin Nigam, the editor of a well-known Urdu magazine *Zamānā* (Time), and a man of refinement and culture who became a lifelong friend and adviser. The four-year stay (1905 - 1909) in Kanpur was highly significant. Dhanpat Rāi here became a member of a literary circle which made it possible for him to have experience of a social and cultural life he did not have before. His writing career had started in Allahabad, perhaps in Chunār, as early as 1901, but now he gained access to a literary organ in which, besides getting his stories and novels published, he could try his hand at criticism, commentary on current affairs, short biographies, and essays. His first novel *Asrār-é-Mābid* (in Hindi *Devasthān-Rahasya*—Mystery of the House of God) had already appeared serially in an Urdu paper of Benaras before he moved to Kanpur. Now he extended his literary interests and wrote essays on Queen Victoria, Rājā Mān Singh, and Gopāl Krishna Gokhalé. He had a keen interest in national and international affairs and covered them in his regular column "The March of Time," for *Zamānā*. This was a crucial period in national affairs and Prem Chand followed the developments very closely. His reputation as a journalist had become so well established in such a short time that in 1907 when Mr. Chintāmani Ghosh, the proprietor of the Indian Press, Allahabad (which also published the Hindi journal *Saraswatī*), contemplated starting an Urdu paper, his choice for editor naturally fell upon Prem Chand. The project unfortunately fizzled out. In 1907 Prem Chand published his third novel, *Kishnā*. The text of it is not available, but it was the first work in the Indian Social Reform League series. Another novel *Premā*, which became later the basis of *Pratigyā* (The Vow), was also published the same year.

Prem Chand's four-year stay in Kanpur was very pleasant and fruitful. He got plenty of time to read, which he did very extensively, and to write. He acquired lifelong friends and interests. He became an active political and social thinker as is shown by his writings in *Zamānā*, which include essays on the Indian religious leader Vivekānanda and on Garibaldi and Mazzini.

But there was another event, more significant than any other. Prem Chand's first marriage had been a disaster, and it is doubtful that it was ever consummated. He had sought solace in an extramarital relationship.[6] In 1906, even though his first wife was alive, he married again. The second wife, Shrivrānī Devī, was a young woman who had become a widow at the age of eleven. She was a modestly educated, intelligent, independent-minded, and brave woman who proved herself a worthy companion for Prem Chand. It took them some time to understand each other, but later she brought a new sense of happiness and fulfillment in his life.

After this eventful stay in Kanpur, he was appointed subdeputy inspector of schools and moved to district Hamīrpur in 1909, taking charge of his new position in Mahobā on 24 June 1909.[7] Prem Chand at this time was a healthy and handsome man of about thirty, strongly built and of a fair complexion, and looked impressive when he went round on his horse on tours of inspection. His travels enabled him to know the country which was rich in historical lore. It had been the kingdom of the Bundelā Rājputs, who in the sixteenth and seventeenth century had put up tough resistance to the great Mughals. Prem Chand's stories written during this period (1909 - 15) mention renowned historical figures like Rājā Hardol and Rānī Sārandhā and have a patriotic fervor. It was owing to some of these stories that he got into trouble with the authorities and had to invent a pseudonym to continue his writing. His duties as an inspector involved extensive traveling and because of the irregular life and the different kinds of food he ate he developed a serious form of dysentery which bothered him throughout his life and ultimately led to his death about thirty years later. Tired of the touring job and to get proper treatment, he requested a transfer and was appointed a teacher in schools, first in Bastī and then at Gorakhpur. He was happier in Gorakhpur than in Bastī because it was a familiar place where he had spent many years as a boy. There was some improvement in his health, the school atmosphere was more congenial, and he had found some good friends. The most distinguished of these was Mr. Mahāvīr Prasād Poddār, a man of deep learning and nobility of character who was editor of a Hindi journal and was later to establish the famous Gītā Press, through which he made Hindu religious classics available at extremely moderate prices. Another was Mr. Raghupati Sahāi "Firāq," a cultured and imaginative young man who was to become a famous Urdu poet. Prem Chand was highly popular both with students and colleagues. A daughter, Kamlā, had been born in 1913; now his first son, Shripat Rāi, was born in Gorakhpur in 1916. His literary work was also proceeding smoothly. *Jalvā-é-Isār* (The Charisma of Sacrifice), which later became the basis of the novel *Vardān* (Benediction), was published in 1912. In 1915 came another collection of short stories, *Prem-Pachīsī* (Prem Chand's Twenty-five), Part I, and in 1917 two other collections. He started work on his new novel *Sevā-Sadan* (The Abode of Service), the publication of which in 1918 established his reputation as the leading Hindi novelist of his time.

Prem Chand was a confirmed nationalist and he had always deeply felt the political subjection of the country. Politics in India had taken on an entirely new complexion with the advent of Mahātmā Gandhi. The era of armchair politicians was coming to an end, and the new politics of nonviolent noncooperation, in which the masses and the lower middle class were taking an increasingly active part, had taken over. The last illusions in the minds of Indian liberals regarding the British sense of justice and fair play were rudely shattered by the Jaliānwālāh Bāgh massacre in April 1919, martial law in the Punjab, and the ruthless suppression of public agitation against the Rowlatt Acts, which authorized imprisonment without trial. In February 1921 Gandhi visited Gorakhpur.[8] Prem Chand attended the public meeting addressed by him, and the influence of Gandhi's personality was electrical. It gave him courage to leave government service though he had worked in it for about twenty years, because he was now convinced of the immorality of cooperating with an authority which was illegitimate and tyrannical.

After resigning his job, he tried his hand at popularizing and selling spinning-wheels which had been chosen by Gandhi as the symbols of India's self-reliance and commitment to freedom. But this was not a great success. At the insistence of his wife Prem Chand now moved to his native village near Benaras; but within three months he received an offer of headmastership of a private school in Kanpur. He gladly accepted it, leaving with his family for Kanpur on 21 June 1921. He was very interested in the activities of the Indian National Congress. But the writing was continued with vigor, and in spite of illness, his own and that of the family, he completed *Premāshram* (The Abode of Love) and sent it off for publication. He had to resign his school job because the manager of the school was a difficult man, but the circle of his admirers was large, and he was immediately offered another teaching job in the Kāshi Vidyāpīth, a national school in Benaras. He also assisted in the editing of the monthly magazine *Maryādā* (Honor) and wrote for the journal *Aa'ja* (To-day).

All these assignments were, however, of a temporary nature. Prem Chand was looking for some means of livelihood which could be more enduring and more satisfying. For a long time he had dreamed of having his own press, so that he could be his own printer and publisher, and start his own paper through which he could share his thoughts with his public and which could become an influential and effective organ of public opinion. But it was a risky venture and he had hesitated to take the plunge by resigning government service. Now he decided to fulfill his ambition. He started a press with a small machine in 1923 and christened it the Saraswatī Press (Saraswatī is the goddess of learning, music and poetry in Hindu mythology). Capital was pooled from his friend "Firāq," and his two brothers; his younger brother Mehtāb Rāi, who was experienced in press work, was persuaded to resign his job and take charge of the press.

Prem Chand had no great talent for business and the press venture, as he himself admitted eleven years later, was "the greatest mistake of [his] life" (*Chitthī-Patrī*, II, 41). It continued as a millstone round his neck till the time of his death, and instead of making any money out of it, he had to take up other jobs from time to time to meet the losses incurred by the press. This was the chief reason for his accepting a position in a film company in 1934.

In 1924 he went to Lucknow as literary assistant in a publishing firm, the Gangā Pustak Mālā (Ganges Book Series). But unable to support himself on the meager salary of one hundred rupees, he came back to Benaras, staying there from September 1925 to February 1927. In February he went to Lucknow again, attracted by the generosity of Munshī Bishan Narāin Bhārgava, proprieter of an established publishing house, the Nawal Kishore Press, and an aristocrat and patron of letters who had great admiration for Prem Chand's work. This stay of five years was pleasant and fruitful. He was given a handsome salary of 200 rupees per month and offered the editorship of the well-known Hindi journal *Mādhurī*. But he had to do some odd jobs too, like writing textbooks for schools, to increase the income of the press, which was running at a loss. In 1931 Munshī Bishan Narāin suddenly died, and the affairs of the press took a turn for the worse. Prem Chand had to resign, but he decided to stay on in Lucknow until April 1932 because his sons were going to school there.

Mādhurī was primarily a literary paper. Moreover, as it was owned by another person, Prem Chand could not express himself in it with full freedom. Therefore, he started his own paper, *Hans* (The Swan), a literary-political monthly which was started in March 1930, almost simultaneously with Gandhi's Dandī march. Prem

Chand commented fearlessly on political developments, coming out openly in favor of the demand for complete independence as distinguished from dominion status. Off and on the publication of the paper had to be suspended because his writings offended the authorities, but Prem Chand heroically continued it. In October 1935 it was taken over by the Hindī Sāhitya Parishad (Hindi Literary Society) as its official organ. It had to be discontinued in 1936 because the Parishad declined to furnish the security demanded by the government. Prem Chand was hurt, and he took back the paper from them. In August 1932 he also took over responsibility for another paper, a weekly called *Jāgaran* (Awakening).

Meanwhile the writing continued, though management of the press was a serious distraction. In 1924 he had published a political play, *Karbalā*, on a religious theme drawn from Islamic history. This was Prem Chand's contribution to the cause of Hindu Muslim unity, but it aroused a great deal of controversy. *Rangabhumī* (The Stage), Prem Chand's own favorite among his novels, was published in January 1925. It was followed by *Kāyākalp* (Metamorphosis) in 1926; *Ahankār* (Pride), based on Anatole France's *Thais,* had been published in 1923. *Nirmalā* was serialized in *Chānd*, a Hindi periodical, from November 1925 to November 1926, and *Pratigyā* (The Vow), based on the earlier *Premā,* from January to November 1927. *Ghaban* (Embezzlement) was published by the Saraswatī Press in 1931. *Karmabhumi* (The Arena), written when the country was aflame with the spirit of rebellion, appeared in 1932, and *Godān* (The Giving of the Cow), Prem Chand's masterpiece and one of the most powerful and disturbing Indian novels ever published, came out in June 1936, the year of his death. During the period of his fatal illness, Prem Chand continued working on another novel, *Mangal-Sutra* (The Auspicious Bond), which remained unfinished. This feverish pace of novel writing went on side by side with the writing of various short stories, essays and analytical commentaries on political, social, economic, cultural, and literary subjects.

Since his return from Lucknow in May 1932 Prem Chand had tried his best to make the press a going concern. But it was deeply in debt; so he accepted an offer from Ajantā Cinetone, a film company in Bombay, to go and work there on a handsome salary. The Bombay stay did not turn out to be very happy. His health deteriorated and he found the work uncongenial. His expectation was that through the medium of film he would be able to reach a wider audience and create some social and moral ferment. But the film producers were interested mainly in making money through cheap entertainment. Prem Chand resigned and came back to Benaras in 1935. He did a lot of traveling and met friends whom he had known so far only through letters. But he was a very sick and tired man by this time. The sickness, his old stomach ailment, continued to grow more and more serious, and he died quietly on 8 October 1936.

Some public recognition came to Prem Chand during the last ten years of his life. In 1927 he was nominated by the government to the membership of the Hindusthānī Academy. The government had inquired whether he would like titles like "Rāi Sāhib." He attended meetings of the Hindī Sāhitya Sammélan (Hindi Literary Conference), and those who knew him treated him with great respect. His high idealism and deep social concern had won great admiration from the younger generation of writers, both Hindi and Urdu, who believed that literature should have a social purpose. They honored him by electing him president of the Progressive Writers' Association in April 1936. But this was a small group. It is an indication of the poor cultural and moral health of Indian society that Prem Chand was never given a place of honor in the social or literary world which did justice to his stature as the greatest living Hindi-Urdu novelist. There were hardly fifty people at his funeral in Benaras. Prem Chand had asked many disturbing questions during his life; the question he asked at the time of his death was perhaps the most disturbing of all: do Indians have a right to call themselves a civilized nation?

CHAPTER 2

Character, Personality and Thought

I *Character*

DURING his last illness, which was to prove fatal, Prem Chand confided to his wife that he had had relations with another woman before their marriage and also for some time after.[1] He had also broken with his first wife though he had continued to support her till the end. The cause of these lapses on Prem Chand's part was the tragedy of his first marriage which was totally incompatible. But, from another point of view, they almost seemed to be an unpleasant necessity to show that he was after all human. Because, apart from these lapses and the moral failure which they might constitute, Prem Chand's character was noble and immaculate. He probably never did a dishonorable thing in his whole life. He was a man of unimpeachable integrity and honesty who had a high sense of duty and honor. His entire life was a saga of hard work and sacrifice—sacrifice for his family, his friends, and his country. His unassuming modesty and stark simplicity were in the best traditions of Indian culture. He was so totally sincere, honest, and unpretentious that his friend and admirer Jainéndra, himself an eminent Hindi novelist, was pained and exasperated. Such extreme honesty was impractical, unworldly: "One needs to be a little artificial in the world too; this is not a place where one can afford to be entirely open and warmhearted."[2] It was because of this uncommon simplicity that Prem Chand failed to give the impression of being a great writer. It accounted for his neglect and his not getting public recognition and respect which ought to have been his had he been a bit more worldly.

Prem Chand was born in a *Kāyastha* family. The *Kāyasthas* (Scribes or Writers) were people who generally took white-collar jobs like those of clerks, stewards, petition writers, secretaries, etc. The more successful ones became lawyers, teachers, professors, and administrators, sometimes occupying high positions in the civil service like those of district collectors, judges and advisers to British governors. But Prem Chand came from such a poor family in a small village that his people were hardly distinguishable from the peasantry. His father owned some land but it was so little that he had to take up a job in the post office. Being men who mostly make their living by "service" occupations, the *Kāyasthas* have acquired a certain astuteness and cleverness, a passion for succeeding and getting along in the world, and an eye for the main chance. But though he was a *Kāyastha* (hence known as "Munshī"), these traits were completely absent in Prem Chand. He had a cordial contempt for what the world called success and placed a higher value on service and adherence to principle. Writing to Banārsīdās Chaturvedī, he said: "I have no great ambitions regarding my two sons. I simply wish that they be honest, truthful, and steadfast. I hate children who are pleasure loving, rich, and sycophantic" (*Chitthī-Patrī*, II, 77).

Prem Chand was of medium height, thin but muscular, with a wide forehead, big eyes, regular and handsome features. His appearance was not impressive, but it was attractive because his kindliness and good nature shone in his eyes. No art was employed to heighten the gifts of nature. His garb was of the simplest—in earlier days when he was in government service he wore a white turban but later this was discarded in favor of a Gandhi cap or he went bareheaded, clad in a *kurtā* (long loose shirt) and *dhotī* (unstitched lower garment). Sometimes he wore cheap canvas shoes—often with missing or untied laces—sometimes *chappals* or sandals. The carelessness about appearance or self could go so far that once "half of the right heel had to be lopped off owing to the deep wound made by a nail in his sandals" (*Life*, 367). In the words of Jainéndra, "The most outstanding quality of Prem Chand's personality was that he was ordinary in every way. Thus he was representative of the people and of the common man. Everyone wants to be uncommon; no one wants to be like the common people by being one of them. But this, as it were, was Prem Chand's sole endeavour, for which a man like me can never be too grateful to him."[3] Indian society has always been extremely hierarchical. The feudal mentality, was, however, reinforced by the long spell of foreign rule so that every Indian who was something was at pains to demonstrate that he was above the rabble. Prem Chand detested this arrogance of the so-called educated elite. His ordinariness of dress and deportment was thus as significant a gesture of protest against this arrogance and an expression of his solidarity with the common people as the simple garb of Mahātmā Gandhi. The difference perhaps was that whereas in the case of Gandhi it was a gesture, a deliberate act, it came quite naturally to Prem Chand.

Though he was a man of strong convictions and firm adherence to principle, Prem Chand never tried to impose his individuality on others. "He never carried his ego and the thought of its weight with him. He was light, easy to mix and assimilate. Not that he had no perception of propriety and good manners. Actually he had a strong dislike of bad manners. But he moved about making himself so light and insignificant, almost like a cipher, that the other person was made to realize the breach of good manners himself. There was no need for him to point out the lapse."[4] But he bore no grudges for slights or insults; he was too busy with his work to waste time and energy on such trifles. So remarkable was his disinterestedness and detachment that like the proverbial *yogī* (man of spiritual discipline) described in the *Bhāgwadgītā,* he seemed to be living in this world like a lotus in the water.

And yet Prem Chand was completely and intensely human. He was a lover of society, and cherished his friends. He had a rich sense of humor, and his ringing laughter had earned him the nickname of Bambuk (a man who laughs loudly and a great deal). He was emotional and could be generous to the extent of being swindled by designing knaves. According to Jainéndra, he had a higher conception of human nature than is warranted by facts. That is why whenever he tried to involve himself with society he had to withdraw into himself with a feeling of detachment. If we believe his son and biographer, he was utterly devoid of business sense of any kind though he would have been reluctant to admit it. But in the opinion of another able critic, Rāmvilās Sharmā,[5] Prem Chand was practical-minded—he made enough money to build a house, could give handsome presents to his sons and daughter, and, instead of selling the copyright to his works, kept it himself, which enabled his sons to reap a large profit. However, his attempts to manage the press and run his papers were a series of failures. But these never made him bitter, and he retained to the end his faith in the essential goodness of human nature.

II *Backgrounds and Influences*

The culture of Uttar Pradesh where Prem Chand was born and where he spent his entire life was a composite one. Uttar Pradesh is the land of the sacred rivers of the Hindus—the Ganges, the Jamnā, and the mythical Saraswatī. Most of the important places of pilgrimage are on the banks of these rivers. The great Hindu avatars of Vishnu—Rāma and Krishna—whose glories are celebrated in the epics *Rāmāyana* and *Mahābhārata,* were born in Uttar Pradesh. The province is thus the religious and cultural nucleus of Hinduism. It has produced most of the greatest Sanskrit and Hindi poets like Bhavabhuti, Bharatrihari, Bān Bhatt, Tulsīdās, Surdās, Keshavadās, Kabīr, and, in more recent times, Maithili Sharan Gupta, Mahādevī Varmā, Jai Shankar Prasād, Nirālā; religious teachers and lawgivers like Manu, Yagavalkya, Kapil. Benaras, near which Prem Chand was born, is *the* holy city where it is lucky even to die for it ensures a place in heaven.

But Uttar Pradesh is also the center of Muslim culture. The great Mughals had their capital in Agra, and impressive works of architecture—the Taj Mahal, the Agra Fort, Fatehpur Sikrī—are located in the province. Besides the Mughals, another famous ruling dynasty had its capital in Lucknow. Its rulers were patrons of arts and letters; poetry, painting, music, along with other arts of civilized and luxurious living from kite flying to falconry flourished at the court of pleasure-loving rulers like Nawāb Wājid Alī Shāh. These Shiā rulers of Oudh claimed kinship with the ruling dynasty of Persia and so Persian influence was even more dominant here than in the rest of Northern India.

Culture too depends upon political power. Though Uttar Pradesh was at one time the hub of Hindu culture, the Hindus, except for some regions like Rajasthan and those under the Marathās, had ceased to be an effective political force in Northern India. The culture of the higher classes had therefore, owing to the political hegemony of the Muslim rulers, also become Muslim. Persian was the court language as well as the language of polite society. This was true even of the Marathās though they represented a Hindu resurgence and were inimical to Muslim power.

Prem Chand's early education was entirely in Persian and Urdu. His early writings were also in Urdu. He long retained the habit of writing the first draft of his novels in Urdu and preparing a Hindi version later. *Kāyākalp* (Metamorphosis), whose composition began in April 1924, was the first novel to be originally written in Hindi. He was well read in the classics of Persian literature, retained a deep love for them throughout his life and often quoted from them. The literary and social circle in which he moved during his stay in

Kanpur was also permeated with the spirit of Persian culture. His lifelong friend Munshī Dayā Narāin Nigam, who was the editor of the Urdu periodical *Zamānā*, was a man of urbanity and charm. At his house in Kanpur Prem Chand had the opportunity to meet distinguished Urdu litterateurs like Munshī Naubat Rāi "Nazar" and Munshī Durgā Sahāi "Saroor." These contacts with Urdu writers became still wider and included the great philosopher-poet Sir Mohammad Iqbāl. Raghupati Sahāi "Firāq," another famous Urdu poet, was his close friend even as a young man.

Though Prem Chand later acquired a mastery of the Hindi language, his direct acquaintance with the Sanskrit tradition and with the classics of Hindi literature was minimal. He never made a systematic study of the Hindu scriptures. The *Purānās* he read as a school boy were in Urdu translation, made more for their story value than for the religious truths they embodied. It is extremely doubtful that he had read anything of the great Sanskrit poets like Kālidās, Vālmiki, Vedavyās, Bharatrihari, or Bān Bhatt, or that he knew anything of the work of the great Hindu theologians and philosophers like Shankara, Rāmānuj, Vallabh, or of the writings of the Buddhist thinkers. About a year before his death he confessed to Banārsīdās Chaturvedī, who was pressing him to visit Calcutta to preside over the celebrations honoring the great Hindi poet Tulsīdās, that he had not read the entire *Rāmcharitmānas* ("Holy Lake of the Deeds of Rāma"; Hindi epic based on Vālmiki's *Rāmāyana,* which is in Sanskrit): "This confession is shameful, but it is true" (*Chitthī-Patrī,* II 90). And it seems amazing to me that Prem Chand should have been friendly with Mahāvir Prasād Poddār, the founder of Gītā Press, Gorakhpur, the renowned publishing house of Hindu religious literature, and should have never said a word about the wonderful work that was being done by Poddār nor mention any discussion on religious issues that he might have had with him. In course of time Prem Chand developed closer links with men who had been nurtured in the Sanskrit tradition—men like Jainéndra Kumār, Banārsīdās Chaturvedī, the poet Jai Shankar Prasād, and the poetess Mahādevī Varmā. He also became involved with the Hindi Sāhitya Sammélan (Hindi Literary Conference) and the Rāshtra-Bhāshā Prachār Samiti (Society for the Propagation of the National Language).

Though elementary education in many places and, particularly in the villages, was still in the hands of Pandits and Maulavis, an extensive network of schools which taught English and provided instruction in modern subjects like history, geography, mathematics, physics and chemistry, and the vernaculars had been established in British India by the last quarter of the nineteenth century. Lord William Bentinck had accepted in 1835 Macaulay's recommendation that English be the medium and English literature and science be the material of instruction in advanced schools. And in the 1850s Lord Dalhousie set out to establish a countrywide system of education in accordance with Sir Charles Wood's memorable despatch dated 19 July 1854. The actions of the government were complemented by the efforts of missionaries like William Carey. Prem Chand himself was educated in the Mission School and, on passing the eighth grade, moved to Queen's College, Benaras, at which he matriculated in 1898. He was very keen on higher education and had ambitions to become a lawyer. But his application for admission to Hindu College, Benaras, was unsuccessful because of weakness in mathematics. However, impelled by the necessity to improve his qualifications, both to rise in his profession and to educate himself better, he passed the intermediate examination in 1916 and the B.A. examination in 1919. English and history were his chosen subjects in both these examinations.

But though Prem Chand's formal education in English was not at a very high level, he was an avid reader and took immense pains to educate himself. His interests were wide and he tried to acquire a good knowledge of not only the political but also the social, economic, and cultural developments in the West. He had a fairly good knowledge of English literature, particularly the novelists in whom he had a professional interest. European writers with whose work he shows familiarity are Anatole France, Romain Rolland, Victor Hugo, Tolstoy, and Gorki. He adapted and translated into Hindi stories of Tolstoy, Galsworthy's *Strife*, Anatole France's *Thais*, George Eliot's *Silas Marner*, Dickens' *The Story of Richard Doubledick*, Oscar Wilde's *Canterville Ghost*, Maeterlinck's *Sightless*, and Hendrik van Loon's *The Story of Mankind*.

Prem Chand stands at the meeting point of two cultures—the aristocratic, Persian-inspired culture which had dominated Indian society since the time of the Mughals, and the new culture of the English-educated elite which would lead them to extol everything belonging to the West and to look down on everything Indian. Politically and socially a change was taking place which manifested itself in a dissatisfaction with the feudal, hierarchical, and deferential society of the past and the growth of a more egalitarian outlook.

It developed as a reaction against foreign domination and was inspired by the new spirit of national dignity and individual self-respect. Thus in spite of being steeped in Persian culture and his own admission that he was "a man of the old school" (*Chitthī-Patrī*, II, 13), Prem Chand was proud and unbending. There are several stories of his skirmishes with English officers when he was in government service.

Prem Chand was a keen student of history and, like many thoughtful Indians who were engaged in intense self-examination to find out why their great country had become a victim of foreign domination, he reflected on the rise and fall of nations. But unlike most of his countrymen who, to escape from the painful reality of the present, were taking shelter in a sentimental glorification of the past, he tried to look at the past in a critical way. He regarded the past not as an ideal but as a starting point to discover our roots. History to him was not something to be idealized but to be learned from: "From history we ought to learn not what we were but also what we could have been. Often we have to forget history. The past cannot become the custodian of our future" (*Kuch Vichār* (Some Thoughts), 71). Study of history enables us to assess our strengths as well as our weaknesses. From it we learn that the common people of our country whose exploits form no part of chronicles have a beauty and strength in their lives which puts to shame the impressive monuments built by kings and emperors. Though they are poor and illiterate, they are sensible and wise. Their lives are full of selflessness and sacrifice, humanity and high-mindedness. Though their bodies are puny, their souls are large. Even more than from the pages of history, literature, or mythology, Prem Chand learned these truths from the day-to-day life of the people. But one cannot accept Hans Rāj "Rahbar's" conclusion that "Prem Chand always condemned whatever was old and hide-bound by tradition; he upheld whatever was new and progressive."[6] He was deeply conservative in many ways, as we shall have occasion to see. He made a careful attempt to discover what was vital in the Indian tradition and critically examined the new.

III *Religious and Cultural Ideas: East and West*

Prem Chand's critical outlook is evident in his attitude to the West. He was deeply influenced by its scientific and rational spirit though he disapproved of its self-regarding individualism and its political and economic philosophy based on personal and national aggrandizement. It was mainly his introduction to Western thought which increased his impatience with the Indian religious and intellectual tradition, because the latter made no provision for change and had consequently become stagnant and moribund. The Hindu religion was full of hypocrisy and superstition, being utterly incapable of giving spiritual sustenance or moral guidance either to the individual or to society. The social structure it gave sanction to was based on exploitation and injustice and a complete disregard of the individual's rights as a human being. Prem Chand was a kind and decent man with a highly sensitive social conscience. To him the value of an institution—religious, social, or political—depended on what it had done to improve the lot of the common man. "The greatness and distinction of any religion," he said, "consists in these: to what extent does it make a man more sympathetic to another man; how exalted is the ideal of humanity which it projects; and to what extent is this ideal actually translated into action" (*Kuch Vichār*, 82). We cannot blame him therefore for his anger against Hinduism. Hinduism had proved itself unworthy of any respect because of the vicious and corrupt social system it supported. True, all organized religions are corrupt, more or less; but there are, in other religions, voices of protest which call for reform of the system by drawing attention to the original teachings of the founders. Hinduism too had encountered voices of protest: Buddhism and Jainism could be termed as such and also the Bhakti (devotion to a personal God) movement in the fifteenth and sixteenth centuries. But while the concern of the former was more with doctrinal matters than with humanitarian issues, the latter was too self-denying, decent, and mild to compel the privileged classes to change their ways. The result was that the oppressive structure of Hindu society had stayed intact for more than three thousand years with its inevitable moral and social consequences.

The Ārya Samāj, founded by Swāmī Dayānand Saraswatī in 1875, was one of the movements which had emphasized social and moral reform and Prem Chand was naturally attracted to it. Critics are sharply divided on the actual extent of the Samāj's influence on him. Manmath Nāth Gupta, at one extreme, discounts this influence altogether, saying that reform at this time in India was in the air and that Prem Chand did not have to be beholden to any particular organization to awake and enlighten him.[7] At the other extreme, there are critics like Shāntipriya Dwivedī, Lakshmī

Narāyan Gupta, and Krishna Chandra Pāndey who emphasize the magnitude of the influence.[8] It is, however, undeniable that Prem Chand retained some form of association with the Samāj practically throughout his life. It is certain that he was a member in 1913 and was regularly paying his subscription.[9] During the period of his stay in Mahobā (1909 - 14), Christian missionaries were very active and were converting poor Hindus. The Samāj had sent its own ministers to stop these conversions. These ministers—Maulavī Mahesh Prasād and his two colleagues—were guests of Prem Chand for a week and had long discussions with him.[10] In his story *Khoon Safed* (White Blood, 1914) he criticized the narrow-minded attitude of the Hindus which was throwing their coreligionists into the lap of the missionaries. And in the last year of his life, presiding over the annual meeting of the Ārya Language Conference held under the auspices of the Samāj in Lahore, he paid a handsome tribute to its contribution: "Perhaps no other organization in India has done as much as the Ārya Samāj to raise the mental and moral level of society."[11]

The Samāj impressed him mainly with its social work, particularly its efforts to alleviate the lot of the Hindu woman. Prem Chand could never be enthusiastic about the strictly religious aspects of the movement with its emphasis on the Vedas as the word of God (very similar to the Protestant theory of the plenary inspiration of the Bible) and its strict formalism and ritualism. In fact, Prem Chand did not think much of the Ārya Samāj as a religious movement and regarded it primarily as a cultural and social one.[12] The Samāj made him more vividly aware of his identity as a Hindu. This is significant because neither by family tradition nor by education was Prem Chand encouraged to think in this way. Culturally, as he confessed to Mohammed Ākil, he was influenced more by Muslim culture than by Hindu (*Life*, 599). But in 1912 - 13, when he was planning to bring out his weekly paper *Āzād*, he wrote to Nigam: "The title *Hindu* was very appropriate. But some other paper of this name has started coming out in the Punjab. . . . The paper should follow the pattern of the *Comrade*. Policy—Hindu. I have no faith in the Hindusthānī nation any longer and it would be vain to try" (*Chitthī-Patrī*, I, 13). Interest in the Samāj may also have had an impact on his style. Prem Chand showed, as Madan Gopāl points out,[13] a tendency to use a larger proportion of Hindi and Sanskrit words than Persian.

There are, however, definite limits to the influence the Samāj had on Prem Chand. A man of his wide sympathies and enlightened and rational outlook could not long remain under the spell of a movement which was extremely narrow, conservative, and revivalistic in many respects. In spite of its revolutionary rhetoric, its expression of concern for the plight of the untouchables and other oppressed classes was mere lip service. Within a few years of its inception, its natural character asserted itself. It made its peace with the respectable followers of the *Varnāshrama Dharma* (orthodox Hinduism with its four-fold division of an individual's life into stages and of society into castes), becoming the faith of the solid middle class, the upper crust of Hindu society. Prem Chand began to see disturbing marks of bigotry in its militant Hinduism, though in the contemporary situation this militancy could be described as a legitimate reaction to Muslim fanaticism. In 1922 - 23, when the country was troubled by communal riots between Hindus and Muslims, he was more severe on Hindu extremism than on Muslim, and wrote to Nigam expressing his opposition to the *shuddhi* ("purification") of Muslims—originally Hindu Rājputs—who were being reconverted to Hinduism by the Ārya Samāj (*Chitthī-Patrī*, I, 132). An article, "Dearth of Humanity," published in February 1924 and written after deep deliberation, shows how far in advance he was of most of his contemporaries and how courageous and fearless he could be in expressing his views. Most of the communal riots began with the Hindus' anger at the slaughtering of cows by Muslims. This excessive concern of the Hindus for the cow was in Prem Chand's opinion quite silly. "If the Hindus," he wrote, "have still to learn that man is a much more sacred creature than any animal, be it Krishna's cow or Christ's ass, then they have not yet learned even the ABC of civilization. The cow is a blessing for a predominantly agricultural country like India, but aside from the agricultural point of view, she has no other value" (*Vividh Prasang*, II, 354). Mahātmā Gandhi did not go that far in ridiculing the Hindu veneration of the cow but, on the Hindu-Muslim question generally, it is obvious that Prem Chand is speaking Gandhi's language. And I think the active influence of the Ārya Samāj lasted only until he came into contact with Gandhian ideas.

But there may have been another source for Prem Chand's enthusiasm about Hinduism—his awareness of the work of Vivekānand; and it is possible that Vivekānand's impact antedates even that of the Ārya Samāj. The Swāmi's spectacular success at the Parliament of Religions at Chicago in September 1893 had created a stir throughout the country, and he was acclaimed as a great patriot and teacher on his triumphal return in 1897. The brief sketch of his life and work that Prem Chand wrote in 1908 denotes the genuine reverence in which he held the Swāmi. The character of Bālājī in *Vardān* (Benediction, 1920), a Hindi rendering of *Jalvā-é-Isār* (The Charisma of Sacrifice, 1912), which is generally taken to prove Prem Chand's commitment to Hindu ideals under the influence of the Ārya Samāj, is in the opinion of some critics based on Vivekānand. While the Arya Samāj had condemned idol worship, Rāmakrishna and Vivekānand had defended it. Prem Chand's own attitude to idol worship in this novel is not hostile. As Krishna Chandra Pāndey has pointed out,[14] the prayers to the Devī by Suvāmā are answered; she does get a son—Pratāp Chandra—who devotes his life to the service of the country. Vivekānand's stress on the service of the poor and downtrodden as the essence of religion was bound to appeal to Prem Chand. Vivekānand's teaching was also free from the intolerance of other faiths which is noticeable in the Arya Samāj. He and his master accepted all religions as true and recognized Christ and Mohammed as messengers of God.

There was another movement which aroused some interest in Prem Chand. This was Theosophy, particularly in Mrs. Annie Besant's interpretation. It has generally been recognized that the character of Sophia in *Rangabhumi* (The Stage) is based on her. Mrs. Besant revealed to Prem Chand the most attractive side of Hinduism—its spirit of genuine and deep tolerance.[15] Prem Chand, who was an idealist and dreamer, was captivated by Mrs. Besant's pervasive cosmopolitanism and her vision of a world community where peoples of different nationalities and creeds could live in brotherly harmony. He was introduced to Theosophy in Gorakhpur by Ganpat Sahāi, the elder brother of his friend, the poet Raghupati Sahāi "Firāq." He borrowed from Ganpat Sahāi the writings of Madame Blavatsky and Colonel Olcott and kept his interest in Spiritualism by continuing to glance through the works of Sir Oliver Lodge and C. W. Leadbeater (*Life*, 372). This, however, ought not be taken to mean that he was prepared to swallow all the occult lore which was freely tossed about among the Theosophists. He uses the idea of transmigration in his novel *Kāyākalp* (Metamorphosis), but it would not be correct to say that he believed in all this. It is more likely that as an artist he plays around with the notion or makes skillful use of it to make the moral point of the story.

This use of traditional concepts is typical and emphasizes Prem Chand's essential Indianness. Though he claimed to be a freethinker and an atheist,[16] he constantly emphasizes in his imaginative writings the healthy influence of religion as a moral force and often takes recourse to Hindu religious idiom to convey his thoughts and feelings. It appears from his writings that he believed in the doctrine of *karma*, though it could be also said that he was merely making use of this concept to stress his strong belief in man's responsibility for his actions as a rational creature and his conviction of a moral order in the universe. He was firmly persuaded that evil does not prosper and that truth and goodness must triumph in the end. Most evildoers in his novels come to a sad end while the good people, even though they may not succeed in the world, enjoy peace and tranquillity of mind. There were some other aspects of Hindu thought for which he had great admiration. On reading the *Bhāgwadgītā* he was enchanted by Krishna's doctrine of desireless action. "This glory belongs to Lord Krishna alone," he wrote, "that he made a synthesis of involvement and noninvolvement. He gave birth to the ideal of involved noninvolvement and noninvolved involvement. Act, but do not get entangled in it. Action is not bondage; it is the desire of fruit from action which constitutes bondage. Dedicated action, if it is desireless, does not produce bondage; it is the source of peace and joy."[17]

As an acute and perceptive observer of life, Prem Chand was fully appreciative of the role that religion plays in the lives of the common people. One of his most attractive characters who is a genuinely good man—Surdās in *Rangabhumi*—is also a deeply religious man. There are many others who resemble him in their deep commitment to religion. On the contrary, an unscrupulous man like Gyān Shankar in *Premāshram* lacks any genuine faith and is prepared to exploit the religious feelings of others in a cynical way. Prem Chand's realization of the significance of religion comes out in his comment on George Eliot's work. Religion, though not absolutely true, particularly in its supernatural aspects, is useful. Freethought was likely to do more harm than good to the common people: "The work which devotion to principles does for learned men is done by religion for the masses. Faith does not love abstract principles; it shows devotion to prophets."[18]

Thus Prem Chand's mind was independent and critical but his temper was traditional and conservative. He was receptive to new ideas and had imbibed the questioning spirit of Western rationalism and freethought, but he remained fully Indian in his outlook to the end. He admired the Western man's initiative and enterprise, his commitment to work and determination to shape his own destiny. He approved of even his attitude of enjoying life, for the Easterner had almost deliberately turned his into a vale of tears. But he disapproved of the Westerner's obsessive and aggressive individualism which had made him not only selfish and acquisitive but even proud of these traits. For what else was to explain his pride in his material possessions, his empires and dominions? Surely there was something radically wrong with a philosophy of life which showed such scant regard for the lives, liberty, and happiness of other peoples.

The essence of Indian culture, on the contrary, lay in its emphasis on selflessness, on the spirit of service and sacrifice. Indian society was sunk in poverty, ignorance, and superstition, and the average Indian was no less selfish and greedy than his Western counterpart. Still, the former's heart was in the right place. His heroes were not Alexanders and Caesars, Charlemagnes and Napoleons, Rockefellers and Henry Fords but Ashokas and Akbars, Buddhas and Mahāvīrs, Shankars and Rāmānujas, Kabīrs and Nānaks, Gandhis and Nehrus—men who had preferred the arts of peace to the glories of war, who had turned men's thoughts from the sordid concerns of money-making and pursuing pleasures of the senses to higher things. In every case their lives were distinguished by renunciation and sacrifice. "India is in a woefully wretched state," as Prem Chand said, "still, no other people in the world can honour a true saint and Mahātmā (Great Soul) more than Indians can. Here a conqueror who conquers his mind and heart is given much more respect than one who conquers nations and sheds the blood of human beings."[19] No sane man in India could ever think of making a hero of a Ford or a Rockefeller. Doubtless the West had had its Socrates and Jesus, its St. Augustine and St. Thomas Aquinas, but they were superseded by the modern commissars and captains of industry. The West which had established its dominance over the world drew its inspiration not from the former but from the later luminaries of the industrial and militaristic age. Prem Chand's attitude may be regarded as biased, but he was an Indian of his time and had seen more of the ugly side of the West's face than the fair.

However, it would be wrong to conclude that Prem Chand's attitude to the West was wholly biased. Whenever he saw moral greatness there, he appreciated it. He was a great admirer of

Tolstoy, had translated a large number of his important stories into Hindi (the collection *Prem Prabhākar* contains twenty-three stories of Tolstoy), and gave embodiment to his principles in his own novels and short stories, for example, in *Sevā Mārg* (The Path of Service) and *Updesh* (Precept). From Romain Rolland he learned the habit, as an artist, of regular hard work instead of waiting for inspiration. And there is every reason to believe that he respected George Eliot for the high moral tone of her work.

IV *Social and Political Ideas: The Conservative Rebel*

Like most Indians of his generation who had received English education, Prem Chand had felt the impact of Western liberal thought. He had not cared to examine the different political and social theories which base the individual's right to life, liberty, and the pursuit of happiness on inalienable natural rights or the idea of social contract. Prem Chand's liberalism was more in the tradition of the English Utilitarians—Bentham, James and John Stuart Mill—but tempered by the moral idealism of Carlyle, Ruskin, and Tolstoy. He mentions with some respect, in his essay on Gokhalé, the names of Macaulay, John Bright, Charles Bradlaugh, and Sir Stafford Northcote and, among the British Governors-General, those of Lord William Bentinck and Lord Ripon. The essay itself is an indication of Prem Chand's tolerance and fairness. It is obvious that by the time he wrote the essay he had realized the fruitlessness of the type of politics which was practiced by Gokhalé. This was the politics of persuasion and importunity, based on the premise that the English public was fair and justice-loving and that it would agree to give more freedom to India the moment it realized that the Indians deserved it. Gokhalé's earnest and arduous efforts to acquaint the British public with the real conditions in India were postulated on the assumption that the neglect of India by them was because of their ignorance. "Indians now know after long experience," Prem Chand says in the essay, "that it is futile to narrate to the people of England the story of our miseries; if ever our deliverance does come, it will be by our own courage and manliness."[20] However, in spite of this belief, Prem Chand is prepared to pay a handsome tribute to the selfless services of Gokhalé and, along with him, to the contribution of other moderate and liberal leaders like Rām Mohan Roy, Mahādev Govind Rānādé, Dādābhāi Naorojī, and Sir Phīroze Shāh Mehtā. One of the explanations of this willingness may be that Prem Chand himself had passed through this phase of believing in British good faith and sense of justice. There is a candid appreciation in his earliest writings of the benefits British rule had brought to India, though this is hardly ever acknowledged by his critics. It was within the framework of law and order established by the British that it became possible for the advocates of reform to achieve their aims. In *Premā* Amrit Rāi's marriage to the widow Purnā can be solemnized only under the protection of the police who alone can keep under control the reactionary forces who are determined to stop it by calling in the toughs.[21] This phase, however, did not last long. Prem Chand was rapidly becoming disillusioned with the British, and in the division of contemporary opinion between the sympathizers of Gokhalé and Tilak—the soft-liners and the hard-liners—he was squarely on Tilak's side. The excesses of the British in trying to crush the wave of terrorism in Bengal in the wake of the partition of the province was alienating Indian opinion. In August 1908 when a young Bengali boy Khudīrām Bose, accused of terrorism, was sent to the gallows, Prem Chand bought a portrait of him and hung it in his study (*Life*, 98). In 1910 came his own skirmish with authority when he was summoned by the district officer, given a lecture on the virtues of the *Rāj*, and compelled to burn five hundred unsold copies of his collection of short stories *Soz-é-Vatan*, which had been banned.

It is necessary to mention these things here because, rightly or wrongly, Prem Chand's attitude toward Western liberalism was directly conditioned by his image of British rule in India. As his disillusionment with the British grew, he became convinced of the insincerity and hypocrisy of the Western liberal tradition. But important traces of the earlier influence remained. He retained his belief in education and representative institutions, though this belief too came under severe strain sometimes. Like Locke, Hartley, the French *philosophes*, and the English Utilitarians, Prem Chand believed that man is a product of his environment and that heredity does not count for much; like Godwin and Condorcet, he believed that man is "perfectible." "Human character," he wrote, "is neither absolutely black nor absolutely white; it is a curious blend of both colors. If the circumstances are favourable, man becomes like a saint; if they are unfavourable, he becomes a degraded wretch. He is a plaything of his circumstances" (*Premāshram* (The Abode of Love), 422).

He could not, however, go along with the pronounced individualism of the liberal philosophy according to which the good of society is automatically brought about by individuals' pursuing their own good. This philosophy is too self-centered: it is largely responsible for our present social and economic ills because it has made man selfish and acquisitive. On various occasions in his novels, Prem Chand expresses in the manner of a Romantic poet his impatience and even anger at the constraints society has imposed on the individual and thus thwarted his natural development or made his life unhappy. People who are too sensitive to public opinion are sometimes portrayed as weak and lacking in moral strength. But at other times public opinion is shown as having a restraining effect on the excesses of individuals. It exposes hypocrisy and humbug and thus shatters the pride of many, based on caste, status, or money. The incident involving Mātā Dīn, the Brahmin Dātā Dīn's son, and the cobbler woman in *Godān* is very instructive in this respect.

The force of public opinion is symbolic of man's dependence on society. No man, howsoever proud or brave, can entirely disregard public opinion or fail to be affected by it though he might pretend to do so. This only means that no individual can live in isolation from society nor attain his full development in isolation from his fellows. As a matter of fact, salvation of the individual depends on, and is closely bound up with, the salvation of society. It was impossible for Indians to grow up as honest and self-respecting human beings until the Indian nation and Indian society were freed from the degrading subjection to foreign rule and the corrupting influence of an oppressive and decadent social order. Evangelical and humanitarian concerns, as great English Romantics like Blake and Shelley emphasized, are interdependent.

Indian nationalism itself was in a way the product of Western influence. Prem Chand, who was keenly interested in history, had made a careful study of how the smaller states in Europe had struggled to gain their freedom from the great empires. He wrote a biographical sketch of Garibaldi in which he also referred to Mazzini and Cavour and the enthusiastic reception given to Garibaldi during his visits to England and America. He also alluded with respect to the American leaders—Washington, Lincoln, Roosevelt.

These various elements existed as diverse strands in his thought until he came into contact with a man and a philosophy which could knit them into a harmonious whole. These were Gandhi and Gandhism. Here was a political leader who could also command respect for his moral character. Prem Chand was a shrewd judge and had at once recognized the unique distinction of Gandhi. He was impressed by Gandhi's austere simplicity, his willingness to identify himself with the common man, and his dedication to work for the uplift of the depressed and the outcaste, people who had until now virtually been left out of the computations of the Indian political, social, and religious leaders.

Politics to Gandhi was not simply the pursuit of power but an endeavor to totally regenerate the individual and society through moral effort and bold and courageous action. What was needed in a political leader was not a brilliant intellect, extraordinary debating skill, astuteness and cunning but courage, conviction, and, above all, the spirit of selfless service and the capacity to sacrifice one's own personal interest for the common good. These were precisely the ideas that Prem Chand had often thought of on his own. The appeal of Gandhism lay not in its being something novel but in its articulation of, and emphasis on, principles whose importance he had recognized all along. Like himself Gandhi had gone for these principles not to any Western political theorists, though the influence of Ruskin and Tolstoy was there, but essentially to the Indian religious and moral tradition. Gandhism for him was therefore not so much an influence as an affinity, a commitment to similar values and ideals.

Prem Chand, like Gandhi, recognized that India was essentially a rural society and any social and economic philosophy which was realistic had to be based on recognition of this basic fact. Schemes of reconstruction emanating from the West could not be applied to India wholesale. There was also an underlying assumption in the willingness to apply such schemes that everything which came from the West was good and everything which was Indian was bad. Prem Chand was not prepared to accept this line of thinking. The appeal of Gandhism to him lay in its suitability to the particular Indian situation. He disliked a centralized, bureaucratic structure of government in which the people who issued the directives—the bureaucrats in the capital cities—knew little of the men which these directives were going to affect. He also distrusted industrialization because it uprooted men from their familiar surroundings, thus making them rootless and anonymous by depriving them of their identity. It also made them susceptible to the evils which he associated with the industrialized society of the West—pleasure-seeking, drinking, gambling, the treating of women merely as objects of lust. The illiterate beggar Surdās in *Rangabhumi* (The Stage) is, on these matters, a faithful spokesman of his creator.

There was another powerful current of thought flowing at this time. In the wake of the Bolshevik revolution in Russia in 1917, many Indian intellectuals were attracted by Marxist ideas. Prem Chand was an alert individual, keenly interested in social and political issues, and it was impossible that he should remain completely untouched by this new wind of doctrine. As early as 21 December 1919 we find him writing to his friend Nigam: "I have now practically come to accept the validity of Bolshevik principles" (*Chitthī-Patrī*, I, 93). And in *Premāshram*, which was written between May 1918 and February 1920, one of the leading characters, Balrāj, gets a paper which says that it is the peasants who are in power in Russia and which speaks of another country near Russia—Bulgaria—where the peasants have removed the king from the throne and which is now ruled by a council of workers and peasants. Shivrānī Devī mentions a conversation that took place in 1928 in which Prem Chand spoke eloquently of the happenings in Russia. There the rich had been deprived of their wealth and privileges and the poor were happy. "That will be the day of our happiness when the peasants and workers will be in power. I think the average span of life will be doubled" (*In The Home*, 110 - 11). In May 1930 Prem Chand paid a tribute in *Hans* to Maulānā Hasrat Mohānī as an ideal revolutionary, a man of stark simplicity and unquestionable integrity who was also a poet (*Vividh Prasang*, III, 411 - 14). This Maulānā Mohānī was one of the eight Communists who had been tried in the Kanpur Conspiracy Case in 1922. He was also chairman of the reception committee for the Kanpur Conference where, according to one account, the first central committee of the Communist Party of India was constituted.[22] In the *Jāgaran* (Awakening) of 13 August 1933, Prem Chand criticized the long harassment to which the thirty-one Communists and trade unionists arrested in connection with the Meerut Conspiracy Case in 1929 had been subjected (*Vividh Prasang*, II, 193 - 94).

What was the exact nature of the influence Communist thought had on Prem Chand? He was not much of an abstract thinker and could not be expected to be interested a great deal in the philosophical speculations of Marx. Communism itself could mean an ideal, a political movement, a method of analysis, and a way of life. As an ideal it had a profound appeal for Prem Chand who believed firmly in the equality and brotherhood of mankind. As a political movement it could be acceptable insofar as it contributed to the achievement of this ideal. As a method of analysis it could be useful in making us understand the importance of economic factors in the evolution and structure of our society and our world. This is where Prem Chand found Communist theory as formulated by Marx and Lenin most useful. While traditional religious and moral thought had attributed exploitation and injustice in the world to human wickedness and folly, according to Marx these were "the effect of laws of social development which make it inevitable that at a certain stage of history one class, pursuing its interests with varying degrees of rationality, should dispossess and exploit another."[23] Marxism thus propagates the idea of a built-in conflict in society between the haves and have-nots. In spite of Marx's historicism and emphasis on inevitability, in actual practice Marxists cannot help functioning on the basis of the theory of conspiracy—that of the rich to rob the poor. Prem Chand at times gives indications of believing in such a conspiracy. In the essay *Mahājanī Sabhyatā* (Commercial Civilization), published a month before his death, he says: "Human society has been split into two groups. The larger proportion consists of those who toil and sweat; a very small proportion of those who, by virtue of their power and influence, exercise control over the large mass. The first group has no sympathy, not the least consideration of any kind for this large mass. The sole purpose of its existence is to sweat for its masters, to shed blood in their service and one day to say good-bye to the world in silence."[24] By the circumstances of his birth and his lot in life it was natural that Prem Chand's sympathies should be with the poor and that he should display the poor man's detestation of riches. "Hostility toward riches," he openly confessed to Jainéndra Kumār,[25] had been the main inspiration to him in his creative work. And writing to Banārsidās Chaturvedī on 1 December 1935 he said:

It requires a great deal of judgment to know real greatness from imitation. I cannot imagine a great man rolling in wealth. The moment I see a man rich, all his works of art and wisdom are lost upon me. He appears to me to have submitted to the present social order which is based on exploitation of the poor by the rich. Thus any great name not dissociated with mammon [*sic*] does not attract me. It is quite probable this frame of mind may be due to my own failure in life. With a handsome credit balance I might have been just as others are—I could have resisted the temptation. But I am glad nature and fortune have helped me and my lot is cast with the poor. It gives me spiritual relief. (*Chitthī-Patrī*, II, Appendix, pp. 5 - 6. The English is Prem Chand's own.)

The letter is a strange amalgam of the language of Marxism and puritanism. Prem Chand talks of "exploitation" and of "Mammon"; he regards his own poverty as a blessing for it enabled him to resist the "temptation" of being enamored of riches. The whole essay "Commercial Civilization" deplores, in the style of Marx, the turning of life into a marketplace; it expresses concern about human work, human emotions, the human spirit being bought and sold as a commodity.[26] Though it is pervaded by a mood of bitter pessimism, it ends on a note of optimism which also is present in the Persian couplet he uses as an epigraph. The ray of light comes from the West; there is seen the dawn of "a new civilization which has sown with salt the roots of this theatrical (unnatural and stilted) commercialism or capitalism; the basic principle of which is that every man who can produce something by working with his body or his brain can become a highly respected member of society and the State, while the one who struts about as an elite on the toil of others or the accumulated wealth of his ancestors is a most degraded being." The latter has no franchise, and is not deserving even of the rights of citizenship. This new civilization is obviously Marxism, or in its concrete form, the Bolshevism of Russia. "No one," Prem Chand states categorically, "who has humanity, spiritual feeling, dignity and a sense of beauty can ever speak well of a social system which is founded on greed, selfishness and a debilitated mentality." He hails the new civilization which is putting an end to riches and personal property and feels convinced that sooner or later the world will welcome it (*In Memory of Prem Chand*, 257 - 64).

This is strong language and has the ring of conviction. However, at other times, Prem Chand appears as one deeply committed to the moral approach of Gandhi and traditional religion, as in the letter quoted above. It was under the influence of Gandhi that in 1921 he resigned his government job and started distributing the spinning wheel. Most of his essays and comments on current events written between 1921 and the early thirties breathe the spirit of Gandhism. He told his wife that he regarded Gandhi as the greatest man in the world, "the man of destiny" who was to lead India to the promised land.[27] Hansrāj "Rahbar," however, suggests that about 1931 Prem Chand's enthusiasm for Gandhism had begun to evaporate because, after the powerful movement which began with the Salt Satyāgraha and which had galvanized the Indian public, Gandhi's conclusion of the pact with the British Viceroy Lord Irwin came as a great shock to him. As evidence he quotes from his story *Qātil* (The Murderer) in which Dharamvir tells his mother that independence cannot be obtained through picketing and processions. This is like children's play. Children may get a little candy when they weep and cry but real freedom will come only when we are prepared to pay its price.[28] There is truth in "Rahbar's" contention, for the bitterness which pervades the essay "Commercial Civilization" is not usually there in Prem Chand's earlier writings. In another essay published in the *Jāgaran* of 7 August 1933, following the arrest of Gandhi by the government, Prem Chand shows that he believed in the Gandhian technique of nonviolent agitation as a technique, as a policy which Indians had been constrained to adopt because they were "crippled": "*Satyāgraha* is not war just as litigation is not war, or the sulking of the child in the home is not war" (*Vividh Prasang*, II, 191 - 92). However, even before 1931 certain incidents and opinions expressed by Prem Chand cast doubt on his total commitment to Gandhism. It is conveniently forgotten by most critics that Balrāj and Manohar in *Premāshram*, which is supposed to be permeated with the spirit of Gandhism, use violent means to eliminate the tyrant Ghaus Khān. Neither Prem Chand nor any of the "good" characters in the novel utters a single word of disapprobation of their action; in fact they are idolized as heroes and committees are formed for defending them from persecution.

While "Rahbar" sees Prem Chand turning toward realism and scientific socialism after 1931, his friend and admirer Jainéndra notices an increasing moderation in his hostility toward the rich in his last years. Gathering hope from the absence of a definite ideological commitment in *Godān* as evidenced by its open structure, Jainéndra likes to believe that had Prem Chand lived to write for ten more years he would have got over his animosity toward the rich.[29] It would be interesting to speculate whether this animosity would have increased or decreased if Prem Chand had lived for another thirty years and seen the betrayal of the people by the rulers. But, essentially, both "Rahbar" and Jainéndra are right, for both the contrasting strains emphasized by them are present in Prem Chand's thought. He was a mixture of opposites and Jainéndra was rightly puzzled by his agnosticism going along with his belief in palmistry, his vehement assertions that man is the architect of his own fate side by side with his belief in destiny.

Instead of laying him open to the charge of inconsistency or confused thinking, these contradictions show the tension in his mind and give an added attraction to his work. They also make him more representative of his time. Prem Chand, like some other thoughtful

Indians of his generation, had noticed a disturbing similarity between the outlook of the foreign rulers and the Congress elite in their indifference to the interests of the common man. Though he had great faith in the leadership of Gandhi and could state with confidence that the Congress was the organization of the people which stood for a classless society, at other times he realized that most of the leaders came from wealthy families or the affluent professions—landlords, businessmen, lawyers, doctors, professors. These doubts had assailed Jawāharlal Nehru too. Though he could say, writing in the early thirties and in reply to Communist criticism, that the Congress "in spite of its vague *bourgeois* ideology had served a revolutionary purpose," he doubted whether "constituted as it was, [it] was ever likely to adopt a really radical social solution." Finally he conceded that "The Indian National Movement is obviously not a labour or proletarian movement. It is a *bourgeois* movement, as its very name implies, and its objective so far has been, not a change of social order, but political independence."[30] Nehru at least had the awareness of the real character of the Congress and the intellectual honesty to admit it. It caused him concern. But there were others who had no such qualms. In conducting the only "no-rent" campaign under Congress leadership at Bordoloi, Sardar Patel took care to reassure the landlords that the Congress party was mindful of their interests. "The proprietorship of the land," declared Patel, "rests, not with the state, but in the landlords." Gandhi himself contributed to confusion on the issue. At times he spoke vaguely of communal ownership of land but mostly he was in favor of agrarian relations being managed by a community of benign, benevolent, socially responsible landlords. And, as Bhabāni Sen Gupta points out, "in all the resolutions adopted by the Congress faction on the agrarian problem prior to independence, there was hardly any bold, precisely defined program for rehabilitation of the rapidly increasing community of landless labourers." In the *Satyāgraha* organized by the Party in the then Central Provinces in 1928, the man who was asked to direct it was Seth Govind Dās, the wealthiest landlord of the province.[31]

It speaks volumes of Prem Chand's social insight that he was aware of these unpleasant realities. The dismal record of the Congress governments since independence shows his prescience. Whenever the awareness of these realities was sharpest, Prem Chand attempted to break away from Gandhian political and social values, spoke in Marxist language, and was prepared to advocate radical solutions, including the use of violence. But his commitment to the moral approach was very deep and he did not find it easy to do so. The well-known letter to Indranāth Madān provides an interesting illustration of these two warring strains in his mind.

I believe in social evolution, our object being to educate public opinion. Revolution is the failure of saner methods. My ideal society is one giving equal opportunities to all. How is that stage to be reached except by evolution. It is the people's character that is the deciding factor. No social system can flourish unless we are individually uplifted. What fate a revolution may lead us to is doubtful. It may lead us to worse forms of dictatorship denying all personal liberty. I do want to overhaul, but not destroy. If I had some prescience and knew that destruction would lead us to heaven I would not mind destroying even." (*Chitthī-Patrī*, II, Appendix, 2. The English is Prem Chand's own.)

Though he talks of "destruction" in the final sentence, his faith in personal freedom is deep enough to make him fear dictatorship. This fear must have become stronger after the emergence of Fascism in Italy and Nazism in Germany. "That government is ideal," he wrote on 25 December 1933, "in which there are the fewest possible restrictions imposed by the State. . . . On this principle, we are opposed even to compulsory education" (*Vividh Prasang*, III, 479). The way to social salvation was not through governmental interference or mere institutional reform but through reform of the individual.

These inconsistencies in terms of strict doctrine will demonstrate the impossibility of fitting Prem Chand into an ideological framework. The fact is that he was primarily an artist, not a thinker, and his strength lies in his breadth of sympathy and understanding rather than in his capacity for abstract thought. His creative power, in art or thought, came from his capacity to feel, to identify himself with the poor and dispossessed. It was his passion for social justice which led him to accept Gandhism or Marxism as the mood dictated. But his roots were in the Indian tradition, which revered compassion and kindliness, renunciation and sacrifice. He was fascinated by Gandhi because Gandhi embodied, in a callous and amoral world, these noble ideals. Gandhi's central importance was that he was fighting for the freedom of the country and had given the national movement a new vitality and direction. But, along with these, he was a man of high principle who set high store by spiritual values and whose vision of the Indian society would, while freeing it of its evils, enable the country to preserve its traditional values and retain its distinct identity as a nation. In other words, Prem Chand was attracted to him for the same reason that he had earlier been to Tolstoy—not to Tolstoy the artist as such but to "the prophet of personal and social regeneration"[32] who uses art as an instrument of moral awakening. Both Gandhi and Tolstoy had rejected modern civilization and its false values. There is a Rousseauistic strain in Prem Chand—as in Tolstoy and Gandhi—which leads him to believe in the elemental, immemorial wisdom of simple folk, those who have their roots deep in the earth, who have been nurtured and matured by tradition. It is this "inexpressible sense of cosmic orientation, this 'sense of reality,' 'the knowledge of how to live' "[33] which makes Surdās a Tolstoyan character. And it is their emphasis on the moral dimension of life which constitutes the indissoluble bond between Tolstoy, Gandhi, and Prem Chand.

Prem Chand's humane and tolerant vision makes it impossible for him to portray real villains. Most of his evil characters are victims of ignorance and superstition, caught in the blind web of custom or the vicious one of selfishness and greed. Practically all of them can be reformed. This faith in conversion—"change of heart" as he called it—places him close to Gandhi but creates an unbridgeable gap between him and Marx. To Marx's pure rationality all talk of change of heart is foolish and irrelevant, for "a change of heart was necessarily but the substitution of one set of illusions by another."[34] It cannot achieve anything, bring about any worthwhile change in society. To Marx the individual as he is is the product of the social system. To Prem Chand too, in his moments of pure rationalism when he is inspired to make theoretic formulations as in the passage from *Premāshram* quoted above, the individual is entirely the product of the environment. His motive, however, in making these formulations is his humanistic reluctance to apportion blame, to condemn and despise the doer of evil, a version of the Gandhian injunction of hating sin and not the sinner. His working credo is to believe in the individual as the initiator of change, to regard him as the kingpin of the whole social structure. That is why his novels—most of which except *Godān* conclude with the establishment of some ideal utopian community—are not simply the blueprints of a new social order but settings in which the individual carries on his spiritual odyssey and, in doing so, also contributes to the regeneration of the society to which he belongs.

CHAPTER 3

The Novelist's Vocation

I *A Dedicated Spirit*

PREM Chand has left us the outline of one of his unwritten novels. It throws a good deal of light on his outlook and beliefs and his main concerns as a novelist. The outline, which is written in English, is as follows:[1]

Two aspects—an unhappy married life due to difference in outlook and mentality, there is enthusiasm, sacrifice, devotion but also a longing, a yearning for love. The heart is not awakened. There is no spiritual awakening. Wife's sacrifice creates love. Spiritual awakening also comes. The whole outlook changed. The whole atmosphere is purified.

A youth punished for [sic] transportation in a political murder trial. His betrothed and father both are transformed. When he returns he finds them ready to welcome him. All fear vanished.

The details should be worked out—160 pages—First Chapter—The trials and punishment. Price 12.

Second—The betrothed girl was present in the court. She proposes to remain with the father of her fiancé. Her fiancé's farewell letter.

Third—The father subscribed secretly to the fund of the political party and is ready to help in every way.

Fourth—The secret is divulged by one of the party. The police threaten the father but he is adamant. His daughter-in-law encourages him.

Fifth—The daughter-in-law attends a political meeting and is vociferously cheered. She is elected President of the Congress Committee.

Sixth—Lahore Congress. She attends and delivers a speech at Lahore. The resolution for Independence. She supports it in an excellent speech.

Seventh—The ratification. Her efforts to form a Lady Workers' Union successful.

Eighth—Picketing by the lady. And arrest.

Ninth—x x x x x x

This outline should help us in finding an answer to the question of whether Prem Chand is basically a social and political novelist or a novelist of personal and domestic life. It shows, first, Prem Chand's realization that the lives of individuals are influenced, even dominated, by social and political forces; second, it tells us about what "spiritual awakening" means to him. It means commitment to a cause, to something larger than the narrow world of self-interest, the scramble for money, power, and position. Third, the "difference in outlook and mentality" he speaks of is thus the difference between a person who has some higher ideals and dedication to a cause and one who is innocent of such idealistic notions and thinks only in terms of the ordinary things of life—possessions, children, social esteem. Fourth, the society which the novelist tries to portray is an unhappy society. It is, politically, in a state of subjection, suffering under tyranny and injustice where people cannot act as they wish but have to be careful lest they offend authority. It is a society in the grip of fear. Prem Chand, however, is not content merely with drawing a faithful picture of this society and with revealing the problem: he also offers solutions and tries to answer the question of how the emancipation and regeneration of such a society can be brought about. It can happen only through the courage and self-sacrifice of the individuals who are its constituent elements. Thus for Prem Chand, the novelist, delineation of the social situation is important, but the way to "dramatize," to "enact" this delineation is only through representation of the struggle of the individual.

Prem Chand is in The Great Tradition of the Hindi novel, one of "the major novelists who," in the words of F. R. Leavis, "count in the same way as the major poets, in the sense that they not only change the possibilities of the art for practitioners and readers, but that they are significant in terms of that human awareness they promote; awareness of the possibilities of life."[2] As a matter of fact, he is the founder of this tradition in Hindi. His moral temper is very similar to that of the great Victorian novelists and sages—Dickens, Thackeray, George Eliot, Henry James, Carlyle, Ruskin, Arnold—most of whom he knew well through their writings. As the most outstanding Hindi novelist of his time, as a man of simplicity, dedication, and moral courage who had thrown away his worldly prospects in response to the call of the nation, Prem Chand during the last ten years of his life had himself acquired the status of a sage, although no one else could have been less disposed to assume a role of this kind. Though he was mostly ignored by the rich and powerful and though, in the depressed state of the country, few literary men in India could ever achieve the status and authority enjoyed by Carlyle or Tennyson in England or Emerson in America

(Tagore's case is exceptional for, even though he was a great poet, the social position of the Tagore family in Bengal also had a great deal to do with his status), he was looked up to by his fellow writers in Hindi and Urdu in the latter half of his literary career. His enlightened views and daring criticism of the contemporary social order, in which a handful of people were living off the labor of the vast majority, had made him *the* source of inspiration for young and aspiring authors who formed the Progressive Writers' Association and requested Prem Chand to accept its presidentship. His presidential address at the first meeting of the association held in Lucknow in 1936 is the most candid and clear-cut expression of his credo as a novelist and "servant" of literature.

Prem Chand finds Arnold's definition of literature as criticism of life the most acceptable:

> Whether it is in the form of an essay, a story or a poem, it should offer a criticism and analysis of life. That work will be called literature which expresses some truth, the language of which is mature, chaste and beautiful and which has the quality of affecting our minds and hearts. . . . Undoubtedly, the aim of literature is to increase the keenness of our sensibilities. . . . Literature is a mirror of life . . . It reflects on the problems of life as well as offers solutions. . . . The present test of its excellence is that acuteness of experience which produces an awakening in our thoughts and emotions. . . . Literature and moral philosophy have the same objective; there is difference only in their methods of edification. Moral philosophy tries to affect the intellect and the mind through argument and precept; literature has chosen for itself the province of mental states and emotions. . . . The keener the artist's or poet's capacity for experience, the higher and more attractive is his creation. Literature which does not stimulate our good taste, does not satisfy us morally and spiritually, does not produce in us strength and activity, does not awaken our love of beauty—which does not produce in us genuine determination and real strength to overcome difficulties—is useless for us to-day. It does not deserve to be called "literature."[3]

Like Arnold, Prem Chand believes that the role of catering for the moral and spiritual life of man which in the past was fulfilled by religion is now to be performed by literature. He talks vaguely of love of beauty as the artist's distinguishing trait and even makes a distant bow to the doctrine of art for art's sake, conceding that literature falls from its high station when it is used to propagate some political, social, or religious ideology (see "The Novel" in *The*

Aim of Literature, 64). But this ideal of art for art's sake is valid only at a time when the country is prosperous and happy. "When we see that we are enmeshed in the coils of various types of political and social evils, when, whichever way we look, we see frightful scenes of suffering and destitution, hear the heart-rending cries of sorrow—it is impossible that our heart—the heart of any thoughtful human being—will not be moved" (65). Under such circumstances it becomes the duty of the artist to strike a blow for the poor, to fight tyranny and injustice, and to strive for the alleviation of the lot of the dispossessed and downtrodden. For the artist is the conscience of the society, the natural "advocate of humanity, progress and decency" ("Literature and Psychology," *Aim of Literature,* 98). Like Shelley's poet, he is the unacknowledged legislator of the world: "he is our mentor; he awakens our latent humanity; kindles noble sentiments in us; enlarges our vision" (64).

It is this high conception of his art that inspired Prem Chand in his work as a novelist. He kept before himself not simply the example of a social and political critic like Dickens or Thackeray but, in his dedication and sense of mission, he reminds us of Milton and Wordsworth. Like them he was "a dedicated spirit" whose duty it was to serve his Maker through the talent that had been given him. He talked of Vālmiki and Veda Vyās, the authors of the great Indian epics, the *Rāmāyana* and the *Mahābhārata.* The creative talent is a divine gift; the great epic poets had used it for the greater glory of God; Prem Chand was going to use it for the service of mankind. Literature itself is an entity; a treasure which has existed for a long time, being the most valuable part of the spiritual inheritance of mankind; a mighty river which swells as it flows and from the sweet waters of which numberless human beings have drawn moral and spiritual sustenance. It is a privilege to be in the position to add something to this mighty stream, to "serve literature" as Prem Chand liked to say and as many other poets, novelists, and men of letters in India have described their creative endeavour. The literary activity is a devotional activity like that of the musician who is worshipping the goddess Saraswatī, the dancer who is worshipping the god Shiva in his manifestation as Natarāja, the Lord of Dance. It is curious that Prem Chand, in spite of a lack of religious faith, is deeply permeated with the spirit of Indian culture and his whole ethos as a literary artist is dominated by religious imagery and symbols.

II *Evolution as a Novelist:* *The World of Prem Chand's Novels*

Recent criticism has challenged the view, widely held earlier, that Prem Chand had little to inspire and guide him by way of tradition when he started writing at the dawn of the present century. Rāmvilās Sharmā has pointed out that the Hindi novel in the age of Bhārtendu Harish Chandra (1850 - 84) had already started concerning itself with subjects like the anomalies of education in modern society, opposition to social reform by religious obscurantists, and oppression of the people by the British rulers; and that novelists like Bālkrishna Bhatt, Radhākrishna Dās, and Srinivās Dās had written fiction of fairly good quality.[4] On the contrary, critics like Nalin Vilochan Sharmā, who has made a special study of Hindi fiction, believe that these Hindi novelists exercised very little influence on Prem Chand and that his inspiration came chiefly from the English novel probably through, in the beginning, the Bengali novel.[5] While one could readily concede Rāmvilās Sharmā's point that there was a living tradition of the social novel in Hindi, there is not much evidence to prove that Prem Chand was influenced by this tradition or was even fully aware of it when he began his career as a novelist. Sharmā, strangely enough, does not refer to Urdu novelists like Ratan Nāth "Sarshār," Abdul Halīm "Sharar," and Mirzā Rusvā, whose work, on Prem Chand's own admission, constituted the staple of his early reading, besides *Tilism-é-Hoshrubā,* the romances of love, intrigue, and adventure of Devakī Nandan Khatrī, and the historical novels of Bankim Chandra in Urdu translations.[6]

Among all these he reserved his greatest admiration for "Sarshār," who he defended vigorously in one of his essays and whose important work *Fasān-é-Āzād* (The Story of Āzād) he later rendered into Hindi. Prem Chand had been trained in the Persian tradition and most of his early reading and writing was in Urdu. He became interested in Hindi literature only later in life when he found a more eager and wider response to his work by Hindi readers than by those in Urdu. Even then he had little hesitation in acknowledging that he had never made a systematic study of Hindi literature. In a letter to Nigam, written as late as 4 March 1914, he says: "I am not yet sure which style of writing I should adopt. Sometimes I copy Bankim, sometimes follow Āzād. I am reading the stories of Count Tolstoy these days. Since then I am inclined toward him. This is a weakness, what else?" *(Chitthī-Patrī,* I, 29).

There is no mention here of the Hindi novelists Rāmvilās Sharmā speaks of. On the other hand, ample proof exists, even early in his career, of his interest in, and acquaintance with, the English novel and the critics who had written on the art of the novel. In the review article on "Sharar and Sarshār" which he wrote for the Urdu journal *Urdu-é-Moallā* (High-class Urdu) in 1906, after asserting that a knowledge of English fiction is essential for anyone who would write with authority on the Urdu novel, he quotes extensively from Oscar Browning to substantiate his view that "Sarshār" is a better novelist than "Sharar" even though the former does not moralize the way the latter does. "It seems essential to observe here," he says, "that often depiction of an event is itself a moral comment." In other essays he also quotes Walter Besant and refers to Dickens, Thackeray, and George Eliot. "Sarshār's uninhibited banter" Prem Chand argues, "is more effective than the serious sarcasm of Dickens."[7]

A novel is "that story," Prem Chand says here, "which gives a true picture of the age which it depicts—its customs and traditions, manners and morals; which gives no place to supernatural incidents and, if it does, represents them in a way that the public accepts them as true." These were the very qualities the works of Sarshār had and which Prem Chand tried to embody in his own work. The facet of the age which Sarshār portrayed and which Prem Chand noticed in his own was the decadent and corrupt state of Indian society. But by this time India was waking up owing to the impact of the nationalist movement, which meant that it was trying to look at itself in the mirror and noticing the pimples and warts that defaced its once beautiful face. The country was groaning under foreign rule, but this rule was itself a proof of its decline, of the internal rot which had eaten into the foundations of its polity. The first step was therefore to remove the social and religious evils which contributed to its weakness. Prem Chand's novels and stories during the first phase of his literary career (1905 - 1918) deal with these evils—the corruption of organized Hinduism, the pitiable lot of the Hindu woman, the paralyzing tyranny of custom and convention. But there is also another strain. Countries seeking to free themselves from foreign rule have often sought self-assurance from their once glorious past. Prem Chand too takes this course, writing historical novels and stories. But his uniqueness is seen here too. Instead of simply extolling the deeds of heroism and sacrifice which were performed by the martial races among the Hindus like the Rājputs of Rajasthan and Bundel Khand, he brings out their shortcomings too.

However, in spite of his shrewd observation, his approach in these works is more descriptive than analytical. His understanding of social and political issues is not comprehensive and deep, while his attitude to social questions is still largely traditional and narrow. Some of this traditionalism was deeply ingrained and was to continue throughout his life. Kamal Kishore Goyankā created a mild sensation among Prem Chand scholars by his publication of a letter written by Prem Chand to the Rājā of Sitāmau, Dr. Raghubir Sīngh. The letter pertains to the question of remarriage of a Hindu widow, something which Prem Chand as a social reformer would be expected to support as appears from the remarriage of Purnā and Amrit Rāi in the novel *Premā* (1907). In the later version of the novel published under the new title *Pratigyā* (The Vow, 1927), Purnā stays a widow instead of marrying Amrit Rāi, spending the rest of her life in a home for widows. "I had degraded the Hindu woman from her ideal by making her marry," Prem Chand is said to have written to Dr. Singh. "I was young then and the urge for reform was very strong. I did not want to see the book in that form. So I wrote the story making changes in it. You will notice that the beginning of both is different, so is the end. The similarity is only in the names of the characters."[8]

This letter should not come as a complete surprise. Some of Prem Chand's opinions were quite conservative, even orthodox. In most of his writings during the first phase—the story "The Most Priceless Object in the World," the tale *Roothī Rānī*, for instance—there are highly complimentary references to the practice of *satī*, the immolation of Hindu women with their husbands. His views on divorce were also not very enlightened. And his conception of the Hindu woman's duties was extremely idealistic, impractical, and unnatural, particularly in the first phase of his career, as appears from *Vardān*. Prem Chand was a representative thinker and writer, in many ways a product of his age. The nationalism he espouses during this phase of his career is of the brand of Tilak, "The real symbol of the new age,"[9] who told his countrymen: "Fight: don't beg," and of the young terrorists of Bengal who believed that the price of freedom has to be paid in blood. The most priceless object in the world, according to his short story with that title, is "that last drop of blood which is shed in defense of the nation" (*Gupt Dhan* (Hidden Treasure), I, 9). The same kind of fiery patriotism is preached in *Sheikh Makhmoor*, "The Sword of Vikramāditya," "Love of the World and Love of the Country" (based on the life of Mazzini), and *Ālhā*. The tone is didactic and hortatory: Prem Chand has not yet learned to dramatize or enact his message. The craftsmanship is unsure—the stories have loose ends, there is too much reliance on sudden deaths and other accidental factors, while the style is still uncertain and lacks a definite character. In the earliest stories it is saturated with Urdu words of Persian and Arabic origin; in novels like *Vardān* there is an opposite tendency to use Sanskritized Hindi.[10] Prem Chand's main preoccupation, in spite of occasional exhortations to patriotic action, is still with the social abuses which had so grievously damaged and debilitated Hindu society. This phase in his career, characterized by a national consciousness which though intense and restless still looks for inspiration mainly to the past, a social outlook which though imbued with an insistent urge for reform is still distinguished by a marked traditionalism, and an art which though becoming progressively clearer about its goals is still not entirely sure of itself, reaches its culmination in his first great novel *Sevā-Sadan* (The Abode of Service), written in Urdu in 1917 - 18 and translated and published in Hindi in 1918.

During the second phase, which begins with *Premāshram* (The Abode of Love) and which may be said to extend from 1918 to 1926, Prem Chand's vision and outlook expand. The evolution is similar to that of Dickens. In his early novels up to *David Copperfield* (1850), Dickens deals mainly with particular social abuses—the ill-treatment and exploitation of children, the miserable conditions in the workhouses and prisons or the lot of the poor in general. In the novels beginning with *Bleak House* (1852) and *Hard Times* (1854), he starts assailing the whole way of thinking which in his opinion was responsible for most of the insensitivity and heartlessness of his countrymen. *Hard Times* is not about the exploitation of labor by capitalists: it launches a frontal attack on the fundamental tenets of utilitarianism which to some people had acquired the status of self-evident truths, but which betrayed a colossal ignorance of human nature. Prem Chand, for the first time in *Premāshram*, shows this kind of comprehensive intellectual grasp, an understanding of how ideas affect individuals and determine their thoughts and aspirations. Gyān Shankar is his first intellectual hero, in many ways more akin to the characters of George Eliot than Dickens. The psychological insight Prem Chand shows in his portrayal indicates his apprehension of the conflicting cultural forces which were at work in contemporary Indian society—those emanating from the East and the West.[11] There is also a better understanding of the forces at work in politics. Prem Chand's exposure to the philosophical currents of Gandhism and Marxism motivated him to define his own position more clearly. The novels are better appreciated as dramatizations of Prem Chand's own internal struggle to determine his allegiance rather than as fictional embodiments of commitments already made. The struggle itself is interesting and rewarding; it helps him attain a more intelligent grasp of reality. There is, for instance, a better understanding of concepts like justice and truth and a sharper awareness of the dynamics of class relationships. In "The Sword of Vikramāditya" (1911) his concern is with individual justice; in *Premāshram* and *Karmabhumi*, justice has acquired a wider scope. Even in relation to British rule, there is an awareness of its vast ramifications. The problem as conceived now is not simply that of freeing the country of the foreign yoke but also of confronting the powerful vested interests among Indians themselves created by this rule, a part of the Imperial Grand Design unfolded after the suppression of the Great Mutiny of 1857.[12] The first step according to this design was to conciliate the rulers of the Indian states—rājās, mahārājās, and nawābs—and the aristocracy—the *zamindārs, jāgirdars*, and *tāluqdars*, people whose birth and status had given them a commanding position in their own society. The next step was to create a new interest by opening up careers to the middle classes by providing more opportunities for English education and giving priority to the establishment of universities for them over schools for the masses. As a result there were thousands among them clamoring for jobs which, in the economically backward state of the country, the government alone could provide. The larger majority of the products of the new educational system were cringing their way into the lower ranks of the bureaucracy, becoming clerks, stenotypists, accountants, and lower administrative personnel in the police, customs, excise, railways, revenue, and education departments. But a few of them were gaining entry into the higher bureaucracy, including the coveted and prestigious Indian Civil Service, and lucrative professions like law, medicine, and university teaching. It was an amoral world of go-getting, of rank opportunism, with its inevitable accompaniments like toadying, flunkeyism, back-biting, tale-bearing, bribery, and corruption. It initiated a phase of national history which has left a lasting impress on the character of the Indian middle classes. The best civil servant was he who had the least sympathy with his poor, destitute countrymen and who could most ruthlessly manipulate them in the interests of his imperial master. Prem Chand shows an amazing grasp of the character of this class and the portraits he draws of this world of vanity and sycophancy, of arrogance and meanness, are not unworthy of Dickens and Disraeli, of Balzac and Stendhal. He can sometimes be a little indulgent in portraying the old world of the rājās and nawābs, of *zamindārs* and *jāgirdars*, but he is merciless in exposing the opportunism and utter lack of principle of the middle classes. This kind of total commitment to personal aggrandizement strikes him as alien to the Indian tradition; while criticizing them, therefore, Prem Chand glances severely at Western education and culture of which they were, in his opinion, typical products. His close study of these classes brings him the realization that freedom could not be obtained merely through reform and reactivation of the middle classes; what was needed was the awakening, the vitalization of the enormous mass of peasants and workers, particularly those who lived in the villages and who had been oppressed and exploited for hundreds of years.

Another characteristic of his social and political outlook in the second phase is that he has broken out of the mold of resurgent Hinduism and has begun thinking in terms of the nation as a whole. The influence of Gandhi here is obvious. The latter stages of the second phase and the third one (1926 - 28) roughly coincide with the dormancy of Indian politics between the suppression of the Khilāfat Movement (a Pan-Islamic Movement for the retention of the Caliphate in Turkey) by the British in 1922 and the visit of the Simon Commission in February 1928. The élan imparted to the freedom movement by the electrifying personality of Gandhi had started fading by 1922. The Congress leaders were in jail and the forces of reaction, both Hindu and Muslim, were raising their heads. The unity between Hindus and Muslims visible during the active phase of the Khilāfat Movement had vanished and old antagonisms had returned in an intensified form. Whereas only sixteen communal riots had occurred between 1900 and 1920, there were seventy-two between 1923 and 1926.[13] Prem Chand, who was always keenly sensitive to the political situation, was worried and frustrated. The optimism which pervades the novels of the earlier stages of the second phase and which made it possible for him to portray scenes of Hindu-Muslim amity, to lead his stories to a happy resolution through the establishment of utopian communities under the leadership of a "converted" bourgeoisie, is less visible now. Even in *Kāyākalp*, written in 1924 - 26, there is an appreciable change in tone, and Prem Chand seems to be preoccupied with moral and spiritual issues.[14] He devotes a great deal of attention to the communal problem, suggesting ways of reconciling the two communities, which is the main objective of the play *Karbalā* (1924), as of many of the stories written during this phase. The tendency is to look inward, to isolate the moral qualities which go into the making of a leader, as in the character of Chakradhar in *Kāyākalp*, and to unravel the causes which prevent unity and sap the strength of the nation. The sense of disillusionment with politics combined with the insistent demands of an aggressive editor of a women's journal—Rāmrakh Singh Sehgal of *Chānd*—lead him in the third phase to write stories for women and about women.

However, as the national movement gains momentum about 1929, Prem Chand's interest in politics also revives and, in the fourth phase (1929 - 36), he again starts writing novels with a political import. *Ghaban* (Embezzlement), which though published in the beginning of 1931 was most probably completed by the end of 1928,[15] is followed by another political novel *Karmabhumi* (The Arena) in 1932. And he had already started work on his masterpiece, *Godān* (The Giving of the Cow), in 1932, though it was not completed and published till 1936. During these years (1929 - 36) Prem Chand did some vigorous journalism, writing profusely on national and international affairs in the pages of *Hans* and *Jāgaran*, had his brief stint with the film industry in Bombay during which he adapted *Sevā-Sadan*, and wrote the scenario for another film, *Mazdoor* (The Labourer). It was a period of physical and mental stress but also of public recognition and acclaim: Prem Chand's advice was eagerly sought by an increasing number of younger writers and he was invited to inaugurate and preside over important literary and cultural gatherings. He was in his fifties now, a wiser and sadder man who saw no immediate prospect of either the freeing of his country or the lessening of the selfishness and greed of the privileged classes in his society. The indignation at the rapacity of the new economic and social order which oozes from every line of *Mahājanī Sabhyatā* (The Commercial Civilization, 1936) is a reflection of his wisdom and his sadness. And the fragment of a novel *Mangal-Sutra* (The Auspicious Bond) is an enactment of his anguish and frustration, a highly personal spiritual document in which he is asking himself whether, in his idealism and aspiration, he had not been an errant fool and his life a colossal waste.

CHAPTER 4

Novels and Short Stories of the First Phase, 1905 - 18

I Mystery of the House of God: *Priestly Corruption*

PREM Chand's first available novel is *Devasthān-Rahasya* (Mystery of the House of God). It was published in serial form in the Urdu weekly *Avāz-é-Khalk* (The Voice of the World), the first installment appearing on 8 October 1903.[1] It is a story about the corruption of the Hindu priestly class. A Brahmin priest, Trilokī Nāth, takes drugs, dallies with dancing girls, and carries on a liaison with a pretty young woman of good family who visits the temple. Involvement with the crafty and lecherous priest finally leads to the young woman's loss of all her gold ornaments.

Actually it does not deserve to be called a novel. There is no story worth the name, no plot, no characterization. It is crude and melodramatic—the young dancing girl, only fifteen years old, hits the middle-aged priest on the head and the latter's jeweled cap flies away, making the girl laugh hilariously. The characters are stereotyped and wooden. But Prem Chand is able to present a true picture of the decadence and corruption of the priestly class, side by side with the degradation and poverty of the dancing girls and their male attendants. Such things did exist in Indian society and this in itself was a crying disgrace.

II Premā: *The Primacy of Social Reform*

The second novel *Premā* is a decided improvement. Prem Chand's tone, which was lighthearted in the first, now becomes more serious in keeping with the nature of the theme—the unhappy lot of the Hindu widow. This novel too was first published in Urdu, probably earlier than 1906. The Urdu title was *Hamkhurmā-*

Hamsawāb (Having the Best of Both Worlds), but the Hindi rendering, published in 1907, bore the title *Premā*.[2] Some of Prem Chand's opinions and attitudes expressed in it incline me to believe that it must have been written before 1905, probably in 1904, as Prem Chand himself says.[3]

It is the story of Amrit Rāi, a handsome and cultured young gentleman of means who has practically everything. He is a lawyer by profession, an Anglicized Hindu who has great admiration for Western civilization. He has been engaged for the last five years to Premā, a beautiful and gentle maiden. Amrit Rāi likes and respects Premā—some exchange of letters has been allowed by her parents because Amrit Rāi is too good a match to be missed—but mainly he has agreed to marry her in deference to the wishes of his late father. The even tenor of his life is disturbed by the visit of a reformist leader, a fiery speaker who calls upon young men to give up all for the love of the nation. The "all" does not include wealth and comforts; the call is only for a readiness to accept social reform; in Rāi's case, marrying a widow. And this is what he resolves to do. A widow is therefore made available for him by killing the husband of a beautiful young bride Purnā who had been married only two years and is not encumbered with children. Amrit Rāi's resolution divides the Hindu community in two warring camps—the proreformists, and the antireformists who see any step in the direction of reform as a plot by the foreign rulers to destroy the cultural identity of the Hindus. They have no hesitation in condemning Rāi as a Christian, a synonym in this context for a renegade and an infidel. The marriage is somehow brought about under the protection of the police. The story, however, does not end here. Premā must marry Amrit Rāi; this can be possible only when she qualifies as a widow. So her husband Dān Nāth and Amrit Rāi's wife Purnā are killed, and finally the two lovers marry each other.

It is obvious that the plot is contrived and unnatural and that Prem Chand's didacticism gets the better of him. But the novel has a documentary value. It emphasizes the primacy of social reform as an essential step in the making of the nation, something which was stressed by Indian leaders at this time. Prem Chand's social and political outlook otherwise is quite conventional. He feels no qualms about recognizing the blessings of British rule, an attitude typical of the English-educated Indians before the impact of Tilak. Mr. Walter, the English district commissioner, is portrayed as a good guy. Both he and the police under his command throw their weight in favor of reform. Walter gets Amrit Rāi a hefty donation from the affluent businessmen and lawyers to build his orphanage by holding before the richest businessman the carrot of a title—the Companionship of the British Empire. The irony is telling. These forces of orthodoxy, so violently opposed to Westernization of any sort, have no hesitation in demeaning themselves before the foreign rulers for worldly gain. But the foreign rulers are not so wicked after all. Mr. Walter may be more unique than typical but such persons do exist among the British rulers. He is a great benefactor of the people. He is so good-natured and gentle that he behaves the same way with high or low. All his time is devoted to working for the improvement of the people. A few years ago when there was a terrible outbreak of the plague, Walter Sāhib was visiting the poor peasants in their homes, distributing blankets to them at his own expense. It was his rule never to use English in talking to Indians. And he is broad-minded enough to compliment Amrit Rāi on his true patriotism, collaborating with him in serving the public.

The corruption of the Hindu temples and the priestly class is brought out again but Prem Chand's social conscience is quite at ease. There is no reference to the injustice inherent in the glaring inequalities between the rich and the poor, no hostility to riches: Amrit Rāi can be rich and virtuous at the same time. English education has done no harm to him; in fact it has enlarged his mind and expanded his outlook. He is the first of Prem Chand's idealistic young heroes, perhaps unique in being a beautiful blend of the East and the West. He speaks of the Buddha and Plato in the same breath; he has written a book on *The Greatness of Hinduism* but is well read in the literature of the West; he admires and practices Indian music but also Western art. The atmosphere of the novel is very different from that of stories like "The Most Priceless Object in the World," published only a few years later. Decidedly it is a work of the pre-Tilak era, prior to the partition of Bengal and the terrorist movement there. As a work of art, the novel is slightly better than the previous one but still full of blemishes. The writing is emotional, the plot is unnatural, the characters are fixed, almost stereotyped, being embodiments of virtues and vices, and can be neatly labeled as good and bad.

III *Resurgent Hinduism: Nostalgia for the Past*

There is a marked change in Prem Chand's social and cultural outlook after 1905. This is the period (1905 - 18) when most of his historical tales and *Jalvā-é-Isār* (1912), published eight years later in its Hindi version as *Vardān* (Benediction, 1920), were written, the period during which Prem Chand's vision of a resurgent India was based on a revival of Hindu ideals and values. Several factors contributed to the development of this outlook. One of these was the influence of Tilak who regarded British rule as "a predatory foreign incubus rather than a blessing"[4] and whose militant nationalism had a decidedly Hindu flavor. The second influence was the Ārya Samāj. It is a measure of the high regard in which he held the founder of the movement, Swāmī Dayānand, that in the roster of great names from India's past that he presents in his story *Dhokā* (Misapprehension), the Swāmī is placed alongside the great Shankar, sitting on one side of the Buddha while the Vedantic philosopher sits on the other (*Mānsarovar*, VI, 198). But Prem Chand, like other educated Hindus, was also thrilled by the triumph of Vivekānand in the West. A biographical sketch of him which Prem Chand wrote for the *Zamānā* of May 1908 shows how much he was fascinated by Vivekānand's attractive personality and his refreshingly original interpretation of Hinduism.

Some negative factors also played their part, chief among which was Prem Chand's disillusionment with his Muslim countrymen. Their politics was still that of unquestioning loyalty to the British, of seeking high government offices, deferring to the British masters, and keeping themselves at a safe distance from the new nationalists who were demanding to be treated as equals and clamoring for the country's freedom. "It is highly regrettable," Prem Chand wrote in April 1906 reviewing Maulavī Zakāullāh's *Ain-é-Kaisarī* (Caesar's Law, or Law of the King Emperor) in *Zamānā*, "that the leaders of the Muslim community are still blindly following in the footsteps of Sir Saiyyad Ahmad without taking into account the changed times and circumstances" (*Vividh Prasang*, I, 40). He also noted among the Muslim intellectuals a deeply ingrained sense of bigotry which led them to look down upon and refer with contempt to the religious and social practices of the Hindus. Maulavī Zakāullāh in his book had said that if the British did not intervene the Hindus, left to themselves, would reintroduce the practice of *satī* in every province in India, that human sacrifices were still made to Goddess Kālī even in parts of India which had made the greatest progress in education, and that Hindus still killed their daughters (*Vividh Prasang*, I, 41 - 42). Prem Chand, who wrote mainly in Urdu during the first half of his literary career, had sensed a certain hostility in Muslim literary circles, something which he had also noted in the

Muslims' reluctance to extend due recognition to the genius of "Sarshār" who was a Hindu .[5] These things make it easier to understand his statement to Nigam, in the letter discussing the latter's plan for the Urdu weekly *Āzād,* that he no longer has any faith in the Hindusthānī nation.[6]

While appraising the works produced during this period, it is instructive to reconstruct Prem Chand's philosophy of history which is projected in them. The short stories furnish more significant clues than the novels. In the story *Yeh Merī Mātrabhumi Hai* (This is My Motherland, 1908), an Indian, now ninety years old, comes back to his country after an absence of sixty years in America. He lands at Bombay and sees the cars, trams, and trains and Anglicized Indians smoking pipes, but, amid all these, he fails to find the real India he had left behind sixty years ago; the one he does see is hardly distinguishable from England or America. He goes to his village, notices hundreds of people, but their talk is about the law courts and the police. Lifelessness, worry and gloom are stamped on their faces because they are racked by worldly cares. Their bodies are thin and emaciated, presenting a shocking contrast to the healthy, robust frames and pink faces of the days of his youth. The old gymnasium has been replaced by a ramshackle school in which weak and lifeless children are dozing. Under the old bunyan tree, a symbol of the harmonious and happy rural community where he used to play in boyhood, now sit red-turbaned policemen torturing a famine-stricken man in rags who is howling at the strokes of their lashes. The old inn is still there but it affords no shelter to the poor; instead it is the seat of wine, women, and gambling. But at long last he does succeed in getting a glimpse of the old India—a group of elderly ladies dressed in immaculate white *sāries* is singing a *bhajan* ("hymn") of the poet Surdās, "God, do not consider my failings," while another group of menfolk is proceeding toward the Ganges, chanting God's name. The old man is thrown into a transport of joy; he discards his Western-style clothes and resolves to stay here till it is time for him to die and for his ashes to be immersed in the Ganges.

There is not much of art in this story. It is an allegorical fable pure and simple but is useful for understanding Prem Chand's view of history. The past is wholly good; the present, closely identified with the West, is wholly bad. The same contrast between the old and the new is the theme of another story *Amāvasyā kī-Rātri* (The Moonless Night, 1913), in which the Brahmin Dev Dutt represents the old India, while the physician who refuses to attend to Dev Dutt's dying wife, because the Brahmin has no money to pay him, stands for the new spirit of commercialism. (The physician is a student of political economy which tells him that illness is a foible of the rich and ought to be "taxed" (*Mānsarovar,* VI, 211).) These stories were originally written in Urdu, and Prem Chand's style, which is flamboyant, florid, and rhetorical, shows strong influence of Urdu writers. But the similes are quite revealing, more revealing at times than the commentary. For instance, "the roots of Dev Dutt's house were shaken like the character of a student who goes to an English school" (*Mānsarovar,* VI, 209).

Bundelkhand, the region in central India south of the Ganges between the Jamnā and the Vindyāchal mountains, was rich in historical lore, recalling the exploits of the Bundelā Rājputs who had ruled here from the ninth century till about the eighteenth. The Bundel hero Chhatrasāl is said to have inflicted, in 1680, a severe defeat even on the Mughals. Some of Prem Chand's best stories—*Rājā Hardol, Rānī Sārandhā, Ālhā*—relate to these heroic figures. Some—*Dhokā* (Misapprehension), *Pāp-kā-Agnikund* (The Burning-hole of Sin), *Maryādā-kī-Vedī* (The Altar of Honour)—deal with the life of the Rājputs of Rajasthan. Some others, like *Vikramāditya-kā-Teghā* (The Sword of Vikramāditya) and *Jugnu-kī-Chamak* (The Flash of the Glow-worm), recall the times of Ranjīt Singh and the Rājput traditions followed by the Rānās of Nepal as late as the later half of the nineteenth century. They are romantic tales of chivalry and self-sacrifice. Prem Chand tries to portray in them the glorious traditions of the Hindu race which had survived intact from the past even in "the Dark Night of Indian History" (*Mānsarovar,* VI, 172). Though they belong to the past, they have great significance for the present, acting as reminders of lost greatness but also of folly. The level of the civilization which they unveil is quite high. The Rājput women in *Pāp-kā-Agnikund,* a story placed in Mughal times, are well versed in Sanskrit, spend their time reading Kālīdās and Bhavabhuti; Tulsīdās, Surdās, and Behārī. The ruling prince of Jodhpur, Prithvi Singh, is an accomplished man who, besides being handsome and brave, is also learned, He is a master of many languages and is widely traveled, having visited Iran, Egypt, Siam, and other countries. The Hindu women are brave and noble, honor their husbands like gods, and burn themselves on their funeral pyres as *satīs.* The picture has a dark side too. The Rājput rulers are strange mixtures of magnanimity and meanness. At their best they are proud, brave, and honorable, place duty above pleasure, the community and the nation above self. But they have extremely thin skins; their jealous and vengeful dispositions involve them in fratricidal strife and prove the ruin of the nation. The situation portrayed in *Ālhā* is typical. In the war between the Chandels and Chauhāns, both Rājput clans, out of three hundred thousand warriors who go to battle only three survive. The flower of Rājput chivalry is destroyed, with the result that only untrained novices are left to defend the country when the Muslim invader attacks it soon after. In *Rājā Hardol* Jujhār Singh loses all affection for his brother Hardol Singh because the latter fails to spot him and come running to him barefoot when the former comes back to his state unannounced, and because Jujhār's wife, by mistake, places the silver instead of the golden platter before him. He wants to poison his younger brother, who, to show his loyalty, gladly takes the poison. *Rānī Sārandhā* mirrors the strengths as well as the weaknesses of the Rājputs—their courage and sense of honor but complete disregard of diplomacy and the larger interests of the state. They are splendid relics but utterly unfit to rule and meet the challenges of changing times. The Rājputs, in their clannishness and lack of practical wisdom, are in most ways a true replica of the Indian ruling elite, which led to the subjection of the country and now blocks the way to its true freedom.

IV The Estranged Queen

Roothī-Rānī (The Estranged Queen) is Prem Chand's first historical tale depicting the Rājputs. It was serialized in the *Zamānā* of April, May, and August 1907. According to Madan Gopāl, it was the translation of a Hindi work, probably Devi Prasād's.[7] Neither Amrit Rāi nor any other critic suggests such a possibility, but I find it difficult to state with certainty that it is an original work, not a translation. It has a great deal in common with Prem Chand's other historical tales—his high regard for Rājput women and unreserved glorification of Hindu ideals, including the cruel practice of *satī*. Rānī Umādé, in her bravery, resourcefulness, devotion to her husband, and intense pride, is an earlier sketch of Rānī Sārandhā. But in its use of the regional dialect the tale seems rather unique. Most of the songs and verses are genuine Rājasthānī but some are fake.[8] The striking difference between the two leads me to believe that the fake ones are Prem Chand's invention while the genuine ones have been borrowed by him from someone else. His knowledge of the language and culture of Rajasthan was not wide enough to let him introduce these on his own.

Roothī-Rānī is the romantic story of the marriage and estrangement of the Rājput princess Umādé. She is married to Rājā Māldev, the ruler of Mārwār. The first night when the newly wed bride is waiting to welcome her princely husband, the husband in his drunken state takes her slave girl for the queen herself and retires to her chamber. The queen is enraged and refuses henceforth to have anything to do with her husband. Only once again in their long married life of twenty-seven years does Umādé, at the earnest entreaties of courtiers and friends, agree to receive the Rājā. But his infatuation with the slave girl becomes an obstacle, for the princess is determined not to be trifled with. The Rājā is killed in action, and Umādé demonstrates her faithfulness to the dead prince by becoming *satī* two days after his death.

Even this plain tale is enough to show that Prem Chand was a born storyteller. There is not much effort at characterization, though the princess emerges as a live and credible personality. She will be dutiful and high-minded, will defend her kingdom, and die at the funeral pyre of her husband as demanded by her culture and code of honor. But she will not humiliate herself nor indulge in low intrigue to win him over. She seems to have the storyteller's approval, though at one point he is critical of her obstinacy which makes her the plaything of intriguers.

The story is placed in the sixteenth century in the time of Humāyun and Shér Shāh. Amrit Rāi, the editor, causes a great deal of confusion by transcribing *san* (the Christian era) instead of *samvat* (the Vikram era), thus placing the story fifty-seven years later (*Mangalācharan*, 351). But Prem Chand himself is not quite careful. The date of the wedding is given as *samvat* 1593, but the conquest of Bikāner which came many years later is dated *samvat* 1592 (ibid., 359, 382). The main value of the story is in its portrayal of the life and character of the Rājput princes when the Muslim conquerors were trying to consolidate their hold on Northern India. Their distrust of one another involved them in base intrigues and made them, in spite of their superb valor, easy prey to an invader. The point is brought home through the comment of Bairāmjī of Mertā, himself a living example of treachery: "Dissension and discord among Hindus has ever been the undoing of the nation. It has always meant defeat against aliens" (ibid., 391).

V The Benediction

Vardān (The Benediction, 1920) is the Hindi version of *Jalvā-é-Isār* (The Charisma of Sacrifice), originally published in Urdu in 1912. Opinions differ widely regarding its date of composition. "Rahbar" believes that it was written in 1905 - 06, but Dr. Kamar Rais, the Urdu scholar, thinks that it was written after 1910. Amrit Rāi says that Prem Chand had started working on it in Kanpur but finished it later; he does not say when.[9] It is written in the same vein as the other stories and tales of this period and is saturated with the spirit of Hindu nationalism. Most critics have dismissed it as a work of little value and unworthy of Prem Chand. Obviously Prem Chand must have thought differently, for he took the trouble of preparing a Hindi translation and had no hesitation in publishing it in 1920 when his reputation as a novelist had become well established. The work is not without value from the artistic point of view, and is of great significance to acquaint us with the evolution of his thought and his art. It marks a distinct advance over *Roothī-Rānī* inasmuch as the author is not satisfied with telling an exciting tale but attempts to portray human beings and probe into their motivations. There are also encouraging signs of Prem Chand's developing interest in the India he knew, the India of the villages, filthy, poor, ignorant, and superstitious, but retaining traces of fellowship and love. This interest is, however, peripheral in *Vardān*, Prem Chand's central theme being quite different. It can be stated in the form of a question he seems to be asking himself: Whether, after the more than thousand-year-long dark ages of Indian history, extending practically from the death of Harsha in 647 to the Hindu discovery of the nation in the nineteenth century, during which the Hindus had been insulted, kicked, and trampled upon, anything substantial or vital of their once glorious and much vaunted culture survives? Prem Chand's answer is firmly in the affirmative, and so anxious is he to prove his point that he does not care much for fact or reality.

Jalvā-é-Isār is essentially the sad story of two lovers, Pratāp and Virjan, whose parents are neighbors living in separate portions of the same house but behave like members of one family. The young boy and girl are inseparable companions in childhood and, as they grow up, this companionship turns into love. But according to Hindu traditions children of families so close to each other ought to be brother and sister, not lovers. As soon as Virjan is about fifteen she is married to Kamlācharan, a young lad of sixteen, the son of a well-placed government official but otherwise worthless. Pratāp is hurt very much by this marriage and also annoyed with Virjan for agreeing to it, though the question of her agreement did not arise because she was never consulted. Nevertheless, she acquiesces in it as a dutiful daughter and tries to respect her unworthy husband like a good Hindu wife. She even develops some love for him and he tries to reform himself. However, the earlier habits prove too strong: he becomes involved in an illicit love affair and kills himself while trying to escape from the girl's father. Virjan becomes a widow, starts writing poetry, and instantly wins recognition as a great poet. Meanwhile, Pratāp goes to college, distinguishes himself as a sportsman and speaker, besides being a brilliant student. One night, overcome by the feeling of love, he sets out for Virjan's house. Was not the death of her husband providential so that the two lovers could be united? He enters her house in the dark at night, jumping the back wall and, peeping through the door, sees Virjan working on her poems. All of a sudden a deep sense of the immorality of his action surges up in him and he resolves to become a *sannyāsī* (wandering religious beggar). Fourteen years later this same *sannyāsī*, now grown famous throughout the land as a religious leader under his new name Bālājī, visits Benaras, and Virjan and Suvāmā, Bālājī's mother, have the opportunity to greet him.

But there are other facets of the story. Virjan, feeling guilty that she was not able to return Pratāp's love and make him happy, resolves to do it vicariously through Mādhavī, a poor Brahmin girl who is her protégée. Not knowing that Pratāp had become a *sannyāsī*, she trains Mādhavī to be a worthy wife to him. When the girl, who is thoroughly programmed, learns that Pratāp has become an ascetic, she too decides to follow suit and lead her life as a humble slave of the master. Pratāp's metamorphosis into Bālājī proves to be the fulfillment of the benediction conferred upon Suvāmā that her son would be a patriot.

The curious thing about this novel is that though it is a story of unsuccessful love, Prem Chand's tone is confident and cheerful, the criticism of social abuses like unequal marriages being mild and subdued. The cheerfulness springs from his sense of satisfaction that howsoever severe the trial may be, his high-minded heroes and heroines will always come out with flying colors, thereby demonstrating the strength and vitality of Hindu culture. *Jalvā-é-Isār* (the Urdu title is the more appropriate) is therefore an Indian idyll, a paean of praise, joy, and triumph that Hindu culture is still alive and "kicking." Witness the spirit of sacrifice that its women-goddesses display, the spirit of renunciation that its man-gods possess. The former are in the tradition of Gāndhārī and Sāvitrī, the latter in that of Rāma and Harishchandra.[10] It was the latter's fortitude and steadfastness in the performance of duty which had inspired Prem Chand to write the story.[11] He portrays therefore an ideal world, an organic community in which neighbors live like members of one family, in which the young are respectful and obedient to their elders, the wives worship their husbands like gods, the rich are conscious of their obligations to the poor, while the poor are hardworking and deferential. Hindu culture is the cement of this homogeneous and well-knit society. There are some villains like the moneylender Rāmdeen Pāndey, Zālim Khān, the police inspector who kills Munshī Rādhā Charan, and Kāshī Bhar, the drunken sorcerer, but after the manner of the demons in the epics they come to a sad end.

The human interest of the story comes from Pratāp and Virjan, both torn by the conflict between love and duty, the passions of the heart and the moral imperatives of a high-minded but inflexible puritanical culture. It is an indication of Prem Chand's conservatism that though they suffer under its tyranny they never think of revolting against it or questioning its basic assumptions. He shows skill in portraying Pratāp's character and psychological insight in tracing its evolution—how he passes from self-denial and self-torture to a perverse pleasure in tormenting Sushīlā by telling her of the misdeeds of her son-in-law Kamlācharan; but he is considerate to Virjan and his attitude softens toward Sushīlā too when she becomes gravely ill. Sushīlā's death is narrated with a Dickensian pathos, not without a touch of sentimentality but moving nonetheless. But the novel acquires a more and more unrealistic air as Prem Chand's anxiety to present an ideal makes him lose all respect for reality. Virjan, after Kamlācharan's sensational death, suddenly blossoms into a great poet and the most hyperbolic kind of language is used to describe the quality of her poetry. But the story of Mādhavī is the limit. It is selfish, callous, and cruel of Virjan to program a tender (she is only eleven when the programming begins), trusting, and defenseless girl in this way. This kind of using of another human being to satisfy the frustrations of one's own psyche is a sacrilege to the human entity. It is regrettable that Prem Chand's starry-eyed idealism practically stifles—as elsewhere in his glorification of the practice of *satī*—his otherwise robust humanism.

Mādhavī starts thinking of herself as Pratāp's wedded bride, dreams that Pratāp has become a *sannyāsī*, and becomes an ascetic herself. Pratāp's house is a temple for her; she gets hold of his childhood toys and treats them like sacred relics, and on and on. This is all silly and sentimental, like the usual wish of his characters to fall at somebody's feet and "cry for hours" (*Vardān*, 131, 140). Also, there are serious flaws in the plotting of the novel. All the lost titans meet one another—Bālājī meets Munshī Sanjeevan Lāl in Rishikesh, stays with him for a year, and then the latter takes him to Lake Mānsarovar in the Himalayas to meet his father Munshī Shāligrām who had become a *sannyāsī* when Bālājī (Pratāp) was still a child. The numerous deaths are unnatural and contrived, as is the fire in Bālājī's room which gives Mādhavī the opportunity to talk to him. And Prem Chand's running commentary is distracting and annoying.

Bālājī is supposed to be based on Vivekānand. Certain features in his character suggest the comparison though, as far as we know, it was no unsuccessful love affair which led to Vivekānand's dedication to a religious life. Like Vivekānand, Pratāp is handsome and personable, receives an English education, distinguishes himself at college, is a great orator, and travels widely though not in the West. Both attain glory at the young age of about thirty. Vivekānand imparted to Hinduism the liberal outlook of the West and introduced Western methods of organization. Bālājī to some extent does the same in creating the Bhārat Sabhā (Indian Society) with its core of disciplined and dedicated volunteers whose religious zeal finds concrete expression in social service. The idea of this service is still largely cast in the Hindu mold. It emphasizes cow protection but it also includes uplift of the downtrodden and helping the afflicted. Bālājī's fraternizing with the lower castes brings him into conflict with the forces of reaction and orthodoxy. Prem Chand's Hinduism is thus reformed and revamped but it is Hinduism nonetheless. It is his enthusiasm for this Hinduism and the impossibly high ideals of its culture which spoil *Vardān* as a novel. But whatever the consequences to his work as an artist, it was an essential part of the author's make-up.

VI *Emergence of the Social Critic:* The Abode of Service

Sevā-Sadan (The Abode of Service) is a transitional work, marking Prem Chand's emergence as a serious social critic. Controversy exists regarding its date of composition as well as publication. I favor acceptance of Goyankā's conclusion that the Urdu version was written between December 1916 - January 1917 and September 1917, and that the Hindi version was completed by June 1918, as Prem Chand's letter to Nigam indicates (*Chitthī-Patrī*, I, 69 - 70). Though written in Urdu, it was first published in Hindi by the Hindi Pustak Agency, Calcutta, owned by Mahāvir Prasād Poddār, who must have encouraged Prem Chand's inclination toward Hindi by prompt publication of his work. The date of publication was most likely December 1918 as Goyankā suggests rather than the middle of 1919 as Amrit Rāi believes.[12] Prem Chand was paid five hundred rupees by the Hindi publisher.[13]

Sevā-Sadan is chiefly the story of Suman, a beautiful, intelligent, proud, and spirited girl. Her father Krishna Chandra is a subinspector of police. He has been scrupulously honest throughout his career but is now constrained to accept a bribe to furnish dowry for his marriageable daughter. He is caught and sent to jail for five years. Suman, her younger sister Shāntā, and their mother have to take shelter with their maternal uncle Umạ̄ Nāth in village Amolā. Through his efforts Suman is married to a poor and ugly clerk Gajādhar, whose first wife is dead. The marriage is a disaster. Apart from being proud of her beauty and her higher social status, Suman had been accustomed to a comfortable style of living when her father was an official. Now she has to pass her days in a dark hovel in the city with the stench from the gutter continuously rising to her nostrils. Gajādhar tries to be considerate to her but, on being unable to please her, reacts with anger. Suman is discontented and depressed. The anomalies of the world and of society disturb her. For across the street from her hovel resides a courtesan, Bholī Bāi, much less beautiful and virtuous than herself but living in great comfort, patronized by most of the rich and respectable citizens of the town. The profession of courtesan is an accepted one at this time, and no celebration is regarded as successful unless courtesans are invited to dance and sing. Attending one such celebration at lawyer Padma Singh's house, whose wife is a friendly neighbor, Suman is late in getting back home. There is a fierce argument between husband and wife when Suman, stung by the accusation of infidelity, walks out and Gajādhar shuts the door on her. She seeks refuge in Padma Singh's house which further arouses the suspicion of Gajādhar and leads him to go about maligning the lawyer. Fearing scandal, he asks Suman to leave his house. Down and out and with nowhere else to go, she responds to Bholī's offer of help and stays in her house. She has intentions of making an honest living by working as a seamstress, but Bholī's blandishments and her own vanity and weakness of will make her slide into the life of a courtesan. She does not stay in this profession for more than six months, for through the efforts of Padma Singh and Bābu Vithal Dās, a dedicated social worker, she gives up this life and starts living one of austerity and penitence in a widows' home.

Padma Singh's young nephew Sadan Singh is by a curious coincidence to be married to Suman's younger sister Shāntā. During his stay in town, when Suman was the reigning queen among courtesans, he had been a suppliant for her favors. But when the news of her relationship to Shāntā leaks out and when his father, mad with rage, gives orders for the marriage party to turn back, he raises no objection. When Shāntā's uncle Umā Nāth finds another match for her she objects because, mentally, she had already accepted Sadan as her husband. She makes an earnest entreaty to Padma Singh through a letter, to which the latter responds by coming over and fetching her. When Suman, in the widows' home, learns of Shāntā's aborted marriage and her father's suicide, she decides to end her life and proceeds to the river. But Gajādhar, who is now an anchorite, Swāmī Gajānand, appears on the scene and is able to persuade her to give up the idea. Shāntā is fetched by Padma Singh and put up with Suman in the widows' home. He becomes more active in the cause of rescuing fallen women and his nephew Sadan becomes his ardent supporter. On learning that Suman is no longer a courtesan and is now residing in the widows' home, Sadan decides to call on her. Suman's sharp words condemning him for his cowardice in deserting Shāntā make him resolve to establish himself as a boatman, accept Shāntā as his wife, and take Suman along to live with them. When his father Madan Singh hears of the birth of a grandson, he softens toward his only son and visits him. But Suman's troubles are not yet over. As soon as her past life becomes known, people start shunning Sadan and Shāntā. As a result they too start behaving cruelly toward her. She resolves on suicide a second time but Gajānand appears again and he is able to persuade her to act as a warden of the home for the daughters of prostitutes which he had established through his own efforts. This is the Abode of Service in which the troubled soul of Suman finds peace.

Sevā-Sadan is Prem Chand's first real novel, and the advance he has made since *Vardān* is almost incredible. The actual theme of the novel, according to Rāmvilās Sharmā,[14] is not the problem of prostitution but the subservient state of the Indian woman. It would, however, be still more correct to say that Prem Chand's actual theme is the decadent and enervated state of Hindu society—the selfishness and narrow-mindedness of its elite who have lost all capacity for independent thinking, are slaves to convention, and lack a sense of social solidarity and the comprehensive vision of a dynamic and homogeneous community which will enable it to get rid of outworn and meaningless excrescenses and invigorate it to meet new challenges and move in a forward direction. Some of the Hindu elite like Pandit Madan Singh are decent people—honest, upright, generous, and God-fearing. But they are captives of ideas and conventions which have lost their original meaning and have now become completely ossified. Madan Singh is convinced of the superiority of Brahmins over the entire creation, believes that every custom is ordained by God. He is furious with his younger brother Padma Singh because the latter does not arrange for a party of dancing girls for his son's wedding. Prem Chand brings out the crowning irony of the situation where the man who was so keen to have dancing girls at his son's wedding orders the marriage party to turn back because of the discovery that the bride's elder sister was a dancing girl. Madan Singh's attitude is typical of the leaders of Hindu society in his jealous concern for his own honor but complete lack of concern for the honor of his society. It is questionable whether these leaders have a sense of the community which they are supposed to lead. Their religion and the social system which it sanctions are based on selfishness and fraud, on the compulsory relegation of sizeable sections of the community to a life of destitution and degradation. As such it is inhuman beyond description. There is no place in it for the weak and the unfortunate, be it woman in all her vulnerable forms—young and unmarried, married and dependent, widowed and helpless; or for the man of low caste. A little lapse, the slightest indiscretion, can damn the Hindu woman for life; not only her but anyone who is related to her or who tries to do anything for her.

The conscience of Hindu society is, however, not entirely dead. There are still some people of decency, humanity, and rectitude. They illustrate the nobility of Hindu ideals which constitute the most important element in Indian civilization. It is necessary in this connection to emphasize the significance of Padma Singh's character whch practically all criticism of the novel fails to appreciate.[15] If Suman is the heroine of the novel, Padma Singh is the hero. He is the conscience of Hindu society—thoughtful, sensitive, kind, and noble but weak and wavering. To some extent the weakness itself is really a part of his distinction. For instance, his inability to take a firm stand on the issue of inviting dancing girls to his nephew's wedding springs from consideration for his brother whom he reveres like a father. He is a well-educated, successful, and distinguished lawyer but he trembles to open his mouth before his brother from the village. He treats his nephew as his own son, having no hesitation in reprimanding his wife when she shows the slightest discrimination against Sadan.

Padma Singh represents the enigma of the Hindu mind and, in a larger sense, of Indian civilization. The very things—respect for tradition, for seniority, for age—which have ensured its survival for three thousand years have now become the greatest stumbling blocks in the way of its reformation, regeneration, and advancement. Madan Singh is not talking nonsense when he says that if Indians give up their customs and traditions, they will have to give up their Indianness, their identity as a cultured and proud people. Keeping away the dancing girls from the wedding celebration might be the thin end of the wedge which will rip asunder the rich fabric of Indian civilization!

Prem Chand does not ridicule this observation. He puts it in Madan Singh's mouth because it is the expression of a genuine concern, a concern which was felt by many other Indians of Madan Singh's generation. But Prem Chand makes the point that though the concern is justified, its formulation is misconceived. It is the formulation of a demoralized and frightened people who have lost their self-confidence and élan. In their fear of being submerged and lost, they are clinging to pieces of straw and have lost all sense of discrimination between the vital and the inessential. The spirit of Indian culture, which is humane and compassionate and forbids any sort of violence as the gravest of sins, cannot reside in conventions which are inhuman and cruel to the extreme. The sages who extolled forgiveness as the mark of the truly great could not sanction the harrying and hunting down of a woman through her entire life for one youthful lapse and the ruin of another innocent girl's life who happened to be related to her. Prem Chand also criticizes the application of double standards, one to men and another to women. He brings out the irony of the situation in which those who seek the favors of the fallen woman like Seth Balbhadhra Dās (there is a cutting irony in the name which literally means "the powerful and noble one") continue to be treated as respectable while the woman herself is considered contemptible. Prem Chand's outlook on the problem of prostitution differs from that of Marxist or socialist writers like Shaw. To him the economic motive is not predominant; rather more important is the question of social esteem. What Suman really wants is not money but status; she wants money because in her view money is the surest way of obtaining status. She used to look down upon Bholī Bāi, but when she saw that society showed her more respect than it did to herself she was disturbed and demoralized. She, of course, fails to distinguish between worldly consideration and genuine respect but this is not an uncommon error. Worldly consideration and deference are, moreover, not entirely irrelevant; they reflect on the moral health of a society. They do corrupt young and impressionable minds and, by showing the hypocrisy of their elders and betters whom they are expected to honor and emulate, breed cynicism in them.

Prem Chand's art shows a surprising maturity in his first real novel. As usual he is a master storyteller who captures our interest from the beginning and keeps it till the end. The story proceeds at a rapid pace and with an even rhythm. Events do not happen by themselves: they flow from the characters and their mutual interaction. And the variety of the characters is fascinating, demonstrating Prem Chand's ability to create a real world, being equally at home in village and town, portraying with ease village worthies like Madan Singh and Umā Nāth and city dwellers like Abdul Wafā and Abdul Latīf. There is a highly skillful use of speech and diction to reveal a man's personality. Even type characters like Bābu Vithaldās, Prabhākar Rao, Dr. Shyāmā Charan, and Kunwar Aniruddh Singh are endowed with an individuality which makes them alive. Prem Chand's approach to character is empirical and scientific; his characters are not fixed and static entities but dynamic beings, conditioned by heredity and early environment but also having a capacity to grow and to learn from experience. *Sevā-Sadan*, for instance, may be seen as the story of the education of Suman: how from a proud, self-conscious, and vain girl she grows into a wise, self-denying, and humble person dedicated to the ideal of service. Her shortcomings, very similar to Sadan's in nature and origin, are the result of a defective upbringing: "She had never heard religious discussion, never received religious instruction which plants the seed of contentment in the mind" (18). So she has to learn the hard way, through trial and error in the school of life. But there is no question of her intrinsic goodness and nobility, and an important aspect of the irony in *Sevā-Sadan* emanates from Prem Chand's controlled but steady effort to demonstrate how superior she is, not only in her essential humanity but in her intelligence and queenly dignity, to her judges and tormenters. Prem Chand leaves no doubt about it that Suman never became a prostitute in a real sense; she was merely a courtesan who entertained gentlemen with her music and her conversation. But even in this she was careful and scrupulous. One of the finest sections of the novel pertains to Sadan's courtship of Suman and her deft handling of his advances. Her coolness toward him denotes not the unemotional calculation of the professional hooker but the self-restraint of a fine human being who is not unmindful of her debts. Sadan is strong, athletic, and handsome, a lad of good family who would have been an ideal catch for a woman in Suman's position. In this case even her feelings are involved, for she is in love with him. But he is the nephew of Pandit Padma Singh, the gentleman who had been kind to her. To accept his advances would be to bring disgrace to the family. So Suman controls herself, stifles her love and treats the lad like a sacred trust. Her sense of gratitude and decency stand in sharp contrast to the ingratitude and meanness of Sadan and Shāntā which they show toward her after they are united.

Suman is the focal point of the novel, and the surest way of assessing a character's worth as a human being is to notice his or her attitude to Suman. Those who stand by her are kind and decent people—Padma Singh, his wife Subhadrā, Vithal Dās, and Gajādhar. There are others—Madan Singh, his wife Bhāmā, the servant Jeetan—who, because of their background and upbringing, could not be expected to be broad-minded, and Prem Chand is tolerant toward them. But he mercilessly exposes those who claim to be educated and enlightened and by virtue of their wealth and wisdom claim the leadership of society—the unprincipled hypocrites who are members of the municipal committee and who represent a cross section of the Indian elite, both Hindu and Muslim.

It has been observed that Prem Chand offers no solution to the problem of prostitutes.[16] There is some truth in the observation. It was a difficult problem and no easy solution was in sight. For instance, the question continues to bother us as to what would happen to the daughters of the prostitutes; who would marry them? But

Prem Chand does suggest a solution and it is embodied in the life of Suman. She had sinned and she repents, not merely through thoughts and words but through her actions by devoting herself to a life of service. What more can one do? Even God, who is perfect, does not ask for more; what right has man? But if Suman ought to repent, so should Gajādhar, which he does; and so should Padma Singh, the respectable and thoughtful representative of Hindu society who bore a great deal of responsibility for Suman's downfall.

Sevā-Sadan is a beautiful and powerful novel. Prem Chand's burning anger against social tyranny and injustice which had made the Indian woman's life a veritable hell on earth is transmuted through his art into a thing of beauty. Moralizing and propaganda are there—Prem Chand's insistence on explaining every thought and action of his characters in general terms is annoying and mars the smooth flow of the story. He has not yet mastered the art of easy narrative which we find in *Rangabhumi* and later, at its best, in *Godān*. And we have his familiar sentimental stuff about falling at the feet and crying (repeated six times and three times respectively). There is too much use of coincidence in the plot; Gajādhar becomes a kind of *deus ex machina* who appears at the right moment to arrange for Shāntā's dowry and to save Krishna Chandra and Suman herself, twice, from drowning. But with all these shortcomings, *Sevā-Sadan* is enough to establish Prem Chand's claim as a gifted creative artist who portrays characters with such feeling and intensity that the reader identifies himself with them and begins sharing their joys and sorrows. And he is a powerful social critic who can embody his message effectively in a moral fable.

CHAPTER 5

Novels of the Second Phase, 1918 - 26

I The Abode of Love: *The Canker of Western Culture*

PREMĀSHRAM (The Abode of Love) may be regarded as the first novel of the second phase, a product of Prem Chand's widened social, political and cultural horizon and a more profoundly analytical approach to problems. This novel too was first written in Urdu, probably between May 1918 and March 1920 as Goyankā suggests.[1] The Hindi version, prepared soon afterward, was published by the Hindi Pustak Agency, Calcutta, either toward the end of 1921 or the beginning of 1922; the Urdu version was published in 1928 by the Dārul-Ishaat (Publishing House), Lahore, under the title *Gosh-é-Āfiat* (A Peaceful Corner).

Premāshram, a novel planned on an epical scale like *Middlemarch* and *War and Peace,* is a story of an individual, a family, and a community. The individual is Gyān Shankar, the family that of the Shankars of Kāshi (Benaras), and the community that of the villagers of Lakhanpur, a village twelve miles from Benaras, in whose fortunes the residents of the city also become involved. The Shankar family, whose present condition is symbolized by the dilapidated old mansion in which they reside, was once prosperous and well-known. But owing to mismanagement and extravagance it is now in a depressed state. Three generations of the family are portrayed. The first is represented by Lālā Prabhā Shankar, a kindly but impecunious old gentleman who ran the show in the time of his saintly elder brother Lālā Jatā Shankar; the second, by his five children, and by Prem Shankar and Gyān Shankar, the sons of the late Jatā Shankar; the third, by Māyā Shankar, the son of Gyān Shankar. The story mainly revolves around the two brothers Gyān Shankar and Prem Shankar. Prem Shankar, seeing no prospect of his family's sending him abroad for higher studies, quietly slips out and goes to America. Gyān Shankar, a well-educated, intelligent, ambitious, and ruthless young man, is bent upon restoring the family's earlier magnificence through his own advancement. It is not possible for him to get a high position in government because, as he complains, the family, instead of using its resources to curry favor with the ruling powers, had squandered them on useless social ceremonies like marriages and funerals. He considers it below his dignity to accept a modest job. The only way to advancement is therefore through better management of the *zamindāri* (the right to collect revenue), which he embarks upon doing. He instructs his bailiff Ghaus Khān to tighten the screw on his tenants, the peasants of Lakhanpur, by imposing all sorts of dues and increasing the rents. Ghaus Khān welcomes the opportunity and follows his master's instructions. His tyrannical rule pushes the peasants to rebellion, culminating in his murder at the hands of Balrāj and his father Manohar, the father taking the blame to protect his son. All the villagers are hauled up, and the lawsuit becomes a *cause célèbre* which obliges all the gentry of Benaras to choose sides. The authorities look upon the murder as a dangerous insurrection which they are determined to crush. The peasants and their supporters see it as a legitimate protest against inhuman oppression. Finally, the victory belongs to the people.

Squeezing the peasants of Lakhanpur is not enough to fulfill Gyān Shankar's dreams of grandeur. He is active on other fronts. His father-in-law, Rāi Kamlānand, is a rich aristocrat, a big landowner, whose daughter Gāyatrī is married to another wealthy landowner. Gāyatrī's husband passes away when she is only thirty-five. Gyān Shankar makes her the target of his machinations, first by maneuvering himself into the position of general manager of her vast estates, then laying claim to her affections. He eliminates Rāi Kamlānand by poisoning him. His schemes at first meet with great success but ultimately they end in failure. Gāyatrī, tormented by her conscience for relinquishing her *dharma* (ideal proper conduct, duty) as a widow, commits suicide. Gyān Shankar's son Māyā Shankar, at the very moment of his "coronation" as the ruler of his grandfather's extensive estates, transfers the *zamindāri* of these estates to the peasants themselves, resolving to lead a life of hard work. Gyān Shankar, disappointed and frustrated, commits suicide by drowning himself in the river.

While Gyān Shankar was planning and scheming, his elder brother, Prem Shankar, having returned from America as an agricultural expert, was serving the villagers. He is the chief supporter of the peasants of Lakhanpur in their struggle against oppression. He continues to rise in public estimation and his model farm becomes an *āshram* (a retreat)—the Abode of Love. Quite a few of the elite of Benaras, including Māyā Shankar, settle down here, leading a life of plain living and high thinking, as in Tolstoy's Nuwara Eliya or Gandhi's Sābaramatī Āshram, and residing in loving harmony with the peasants and laborers.

Most criticism of the novel leaves one dissatisfied, as the critics have failed to appreciate Prem Chand's complex vision and his subtle artistry. The inveterate tendency in Hindi criticism to see Prem Chand as first and last a social critic and a "progressive," ignoring other aspects of his work, is perhaps best seen in criticism of this novel. Even two of the ablest critics—Indranāth Madān and Rāmvilās Sharmā—fail to do justice to the novel, though not for lack of enthusiasm. To Madān[2] it is primarily a social novel because it seeks to arouse the people against their exploitation by the *zamindārs*. Sharmā[3] sees it as a great novel, but his emphasis is exclusively on the sociopolitical aspect, with hardly any reference to the moral and cultural issues involved. The fact is that, though *Premāshram* is a social and political novel, the most important dimension of the novel is the cultural and moral one. Even the social criticism is presented in the cultural garb. The main theme is introduced right at the beginning of the novel in the discussion among the illiterate peasants of Lakhanpur. "What is the use of education?" they seem to ask. "In what way is the educated man superior to those who are uneducated? Has he become more human, more just?" The questions are repeated as a leitmotiv throughout the novel. Prabhā Shankar, pained by Gyān Shankar's behavior, reflects: "Education should normally have the effect of making a man more patient and contented, restraining his egoism and making him more generous rather than bringing him under the control of the demon of selfishness, meanness, and unscrupulousness" (38). And one could not conceive a more devastating indictment of the educated elite in India than Kādir Miān's appreciative comment to Prem Shankar:

> During my long life I have seen hundreds of educated men but, except for you, I did not meet a single one who did not cut our throats. The whole world speaks highly of education. It seems to us that education makes a man a greater crook. It teaches people to squeeze the neck of the poor. God gave you true education. That is why other educated people have become hostile to you. (136 - 37)

Intertwined with the theme of education is that of culture, in this case that of the East and West; and the moral one—whether it is possible for a man who is ruthlessly pursuing his self-interest to be happy. There are various other dichotomies which enrich the texture of the novel and illustrate Prem Chand's adroitness and skill in keeping so many issues alive without letting them interfere with the smooth flow of the narrative or the creation of a real world of living human beings. Some of these dichotomies are between the uneducated and educated, East and West, old and new, village and town, emotion and intellect, violence and nonviolence, Marxism and Gandhism, individualism and socialism. Prem Chand's dialectical mind makes him wary of looking at one of these paired principles as the exclusive preserve of goodness and rightness. He does take sides but that does not make him extol or condemn the opposing principle. For instance, he is severe in his criticism of Western cultural values but it does not mean that everything the East represents is praiseworthy.

Like the novels of George Eliot, "the organic form" of Prem Chand's novels consists of "an inner circle (a small group of individuals involved in a moral dilemma) surrounded by an outer circle (the social world within which the dilemma has to be resolved)."[4] The plot of *Premāshram* too moves in two circles. In the inner circle it is the drama of the life of the hero Gyān Shankar and the heroine Gāyatrī; in the outer circle, of the villagers of Lakhanpur in their struggle against the vested interests, both inside and outside the village. Gyān Shankar, whose actions affect the lives of practically all the characters in the novel, is the link between these two worlds.

He is described as a man of great talents and considerable intellectual power. He can think as well as act, being a writer and speaker of distinction and an able administrator. Whatever the challenge, Gyān Shankar never fails to rise to it, sometimes wondering at his own abilities. But his heart is not in the right place. Prem Chand's object is to show how a man so able and intelligent can utterly fail to find happiness in life when he lacks kindness and sympathy.

Gyān Shankar's shortcomings are not the result of a defective biological or social inheritance but of a bad education—the Western system of education which was the gift of the British *Rāj* and which was expected to civilize and enlighten the Indians. It *has* civilized and enlightened them, but also dehumanized them in the process.

They have become clever logicians and skillful men of business but have lost the spirit of self-denial, self-sacrifice, and compassion which constitute the essence of Indian culture. The individual is the focus of the universe in Western liberalism, which has been more appropriately called "possessive individualism."[5] The practical effect of this creed is that it makes a person supremely selfish. All thought is of one's own advancement, irrespective of its effect on others. The collective good in the capitalistic economy, the form of economic organization favored most by possessive individualism, is supposed to be brought about through each individual's pursuing his own good. According to Adam Smith's celebrated theory of the natural identity of interests, the clash between different "goods" is avoided by the interposition of "the hidden hand." The individual therefore does not have to bother about the good of society. It is his right as well as his duty to pursue his own good.

This is exactly what Gyān Shankar does. The thought of anybody else's interests never enters his mind. Wife, brother, friend; love, marriage, religion—every human being, every human relation, is used by him in his relentless pursuit of wealth, power and influence, as an instrument of his own advancement. Nothing is sacred or inviolable. He becomes a devotee of Krishna, the God of Love, so that Gāyatrī can become his sweetheart as Rādhā, the lovelorn milkmaid of Vrindāban. He almost succeeds in his clever scheme, but it is ruined by the untimely intrusion of his wife Vidyā, who is so shocked at her husband's degradation that she dies of a broken heart. But Vidyā's death does not affect Gyān Shankar; he continues to pursue his dreams of grandeur. He achieves a remarkable degree of success, becomes a leading citizen of Lucknow, the secretary of the landlords' association, and is able to get his Excellency the Governor of the United Provinces to "crown" his son Māyā Shankar as the new landlord. But at the very moment of his triumph, the cup turns sour on his lips through Māyā Shankar's great act of renunciation. This renunciation has a significance much greater than the money value of the estates. It is a demonstration of the fact that the gods Gyān Shankar had worshipped throughout his life were false gods, an impossible admission for a man of Gyān Shankar's supreme faith in his own intelligence and cunning. The only recourse for him is suicide.

Gyān Shankar's is a tragic story, developed in the characteristic form of a moral fable. The point which Prem Chand tries to make is that Gyān Shankar is not a foolish or a bad man. Rather he is the victim of a false set of values, the creed of materialism and unrestrained individualism which was being embraced by the educated classes with all the zeal of new converts. Instead of imbuing us with high ideals and instructing us to treat our fellow beings as brothers, this creed had turned education into the fine art of robbing the weak and defenseless. Rāi Kamlānand's parting words to Gyān Shankar (165) are in this respect a faithful echo of Prem Chand's own beliefs. Judged in this light, the uneducated villagers of Lakhanpur are better educated than the so-called elite, for they are the inheritors of a great culture and know the secret of a simple, contented life. Though their lives are riven by petty jealousies, they can forget their differences when occasion demands and can share in one another's joys and sorrows. In spite of centuries of oppression, they have enough intelligence, initiative, industry, and skill to improve their lot, enough talent and imagination to enrich their lives if only their "educated" brethren could remove the hand of oppression and exploitation from above their heads and offer, occasionally, some help, as Prem Shankar does.

However, though the West is vitiated, the East is not perfect. Lālā Prabhā Shankar, with all his gentleness and goodness, is a weak and pathetic creature, utterly helpless in meeting the challenges of the new age. There is no surer proof of his incompetence than his failure to give a proper upbringing to his sons. Shraddhā, Prem Shankar's deeply religious wife, is a devoted Hindu woman but she is sunk in superstition. Rāi Bahādur Kamlānand, a more complex creation, acts at times as the author's surrogate in the novel, but Prem Chand does not approve of him entirely. He is the type of the old aristocrat who, while representing some of the best in Indian culture, also has the aristocracy's sense of realism which makes it come to terms with the ruling power. His intelligence and grasp of reality are impressive, but we have doubts about his courage and willpower, of which he seems to be proud to the point of vanity. Believing that music is a nation's most valuable treasure, he is prepared to spend lakhs of rupees on a musical soirée without concerning himself with the lot of the peasants from whom this money is collected. If compelled to take note of their condition his reply would presumably have been the same as it is to Gyān Shankar in another context: "All creatures in the world obtain happiness or misery according to their *karma* (the effect of former deeds, performed either in this life or in a previous one). I am not the arbiter of anyone's destiny" (166). Through Kamlānand's character Prem Chand exposes the great weakness in traditional Hinduism which, with all its lofty spirituality, has regarded a social conscience as an inconvenient burden.

Premāshram is a work of graphic realism, the vivid portrayal of the life in Lakhanpur village being a vital part of the novel. Prem Chand has no equal among Hindi novelists in the depiction of rural life and invites comparison with his English contemporary Thomas Hardy, with his striking picture of Wessex. But Prem Chand is also a social and political critic. He discloses the reality behind the myth of the British *Rāj* and its legendary system of justice under which the high and low were supposed to be equal before the law. We see the Imperial Grand Design in operation: how the foreign rulers win the loyalty and devotion of the vested interests by giving them complete freedom to ride on the backs of the poor peasants. Prem Chand is lenient to the British—after all they were foreigners—but he is merciless in exposing the selfishness and greed of the Indian elite. His social views, however, do not easily fit into an ideological framework. His approach is eclectic and he is prepared to take elements from disparate and even conflicting ideologies. From communism he takes its regard for the common man and for his right to a decent life. But there is no insistence on equality, no antagonism of classes, not even a thought of the dictatorship of the proletariat. The actual governing is still to be done by the classes which have traditionally enjoyed power and prestige. It is to be a paternalistic society in which an aristocracy of the wise and virtuous provide the leadership which the common people gladly accept. In Prem Chand's utopia, the House of Love, Prem Shankar, who gives the name to the rural commune, is the undisputed leader and governor. He earns his right to govern through his virtues—his selflessness and spirit of renunciation, his love for the poor and downtrodden, his complete freedom from guile, and his willingness to work with his own hands. This sense of the dignity of labor he has acquired during his stay in America. He is also a Gandhian who, like Prem Chand's other idealistic young heroes, abhors violence and stops it by his readiness to sacrifice himself. However, it is necessary to remember that Prem Shankar's position—as that of the intellectuals and professionals who form part of the utopian community—derives also from his social origin. He is the scion of a landowning family, the elder brother of Gyān Shankar. The workers and peasants of the Āshram, as of Lakhanpur, know their places when they meet with the leaders. Their lower status is not only owing to their lack of education and cultivation but also their low social origin in the Hindu-Muslim hierarchy of caste and class. Curiously enough, Prem Chand never questions the existence of this hierarchy, though at times he might question its basis. There is not a single man from the working classes who comes to occupy a position equal to that of the elite. Even Balrāj, who is represented as the most stiff-necked, independent-minded, and audacious of the villagers and who is the actual killer of Ghaus Khān, greets Māyā Shankar by falling at his feet. This falling at the feet, which is a common occurrence in Prem Chand's novels and denotes his sentimentality, has a special significance in the context of this novel. For common though it might be, one can never imagine a man from a higher caste or class falling at the feet of one from a lower caste or class, just as it is difficult to imagine an older man of the same status falling at a younger man's feet. It is essential to draw attention to these points because even distinguished critics like Rāmvilās Sharmā have represented Prem Chand as a very progressive, even a Marxist thinker. But evidence from his work shows that, while he is an original and daring social critic, a rebel, he is not a revolutionary—at least not yet.

There are serious weaknesses in *Premāshram*. Prem Shankar never comes to life and is oddly passive, mostly reacting to events rather than initiating them. It is difficult to accept him as the hero of the novel though it has been named after him. Gyān Shankar is the chief protagonist, but, though he is a striking character, Prem Chand is not able to carry us along with him when he tries to show that he is a man and not a monster. There is a wide gap between description and "enactment": with all the author's special pleading, Gyān Shankar comes very close to being an entirely evil man. Gāyatrī too is vague and unsubstantial. Rāi Kamlānand promises to be lively and exciting, but Prem Chand's eagerness to make him a repository of all the accomplishments he can think of makes him an abstraction. Similarly, none of the women comes to life though Vidyā is three-dimensional. But Lālā Prabhā Shankar is real; so are the peasants of Lakhanpur, who are beings of flesh and blood whom we can feel and touch and the cadence of whose voices we can immediately recognize. They are a living proof of Prem Chand's stature as a great novelist. In spite of some bizarre incidents, like the deaths of Prabhā Shankar's two younger sons in their experiments with the occult, the novel portrays a convincing and real world. The utopian ending weakens it, but "sages" have their problems and Prem Chand undoubtedly had his. After condemning the elite of Indian society so savagely, he could not leave them to think that they were beyond redemption, for the future of the country depended upon them. Prem Chand therefore could conclude the novel only on a note of faith, hope, and love.

II The Stage: *The Gandhian Way*

Rangabhumi (The Stage) is Prem Chand's most ambitious novel, conceived on an epic scale. He paints on a broad canvas. At the top is the world of the rich aristocrats and aspiring industrialists; at the bottom, that of the residents of Pāndépur village. The middle level is rather thinly drawn.

Among the aristocratic families is that of Rājā Bharat Singh, a learned gentleman of retiring habits. His wife Rānī Jānhvī, however, is outgoing and aggressive. The Singhs are idealistic and have organized, under the leadership of their son Vinaya Singh, a group of volunteers to serve the nation. Their daughter Indu, a proud but jealous Rājput lady, has been married to Rājā Mahendra Kumār, an aristocrat of the new stamp who considers himself a servant of the people. He is chairman of the municipal committee and has done good work in that capacity.

The Sevak family is very different in character and outlook. They are Indian Christians who had converted to the religion of Jesus two generations ago, in days following the great Indian revolt of 1857 when any demonstration of loyalty to the *Rāj* was bound to bring quick returns. Opportunism thus runs in their blood. Mrs. Sevak is a narrow-minded and mean-spirited bigot who hates everything Indian. Her natural affinities, she is convinced, are with the English; her cherished desire therefore is to marry her daughter Sophia to Mr. Clark, the English district officer. But Sophia is proud of her Indianness and is attracted by Hindu, Buddhist, and Jain thought. Her brother Prabhu Sevak is a poet and dreamer. Though he had been sent by his father to America to train in cigarette manufacturing and had spent three years there, he has no interest in the work.

At the other end of the social scale are the villagers of Pāndépur, a fairly representative group, including Nāyak Rām, a Brahmin priest; Bajrangī, a cattle owner who sells milk; Jagdhar, a sweets vendor; Bhairon, a liquor seller; and Surdās, a blind beggar of the untouchable class, outwardly a frail, miserable, and pathetic creature.

Rangabhumi, which could mean "the stage" as well as "the arena," is primarily the story of a contest in which the adversaries are unevenly matched. The contest, in its outer circle, takes the form of a confrontation between Surdās and the poor people of Pāndépur and those who are out to dislodge them. In its inner circle, it is a confrontation between Surdās and the residents of the village itself who, in their vanity and self-conceit, try to harass and humiliate the lonely beggar. Surdās triumphs in the end, not materially but morally in that his adversaries in the village as well as outside recognize his nobility and greatness.

Mr. John Sevak, an Indian Christian in his fifties, capable, masterful, and ruthless, wants to establish a cigarette factory on a plot of land near Pāndépur village. The plot is owned by Surdās who, in spite of his grinding poverty, has kept it because it is a patrimony but mainly because it is useful to the villagers as the only grazing ground for their cattle. Like John Sevak he has his own plans for the vacant land—to build a well, a temple, and a *dharamshālā* (an inn where travelers can stay without payment). John Sevak uses every means, fair or foul, to make Surdās sell the land. Surdās refuses, politely but firmly. His objection is that once a factory is put up there, other attendant evils will follow. There will be drinking parlors, gambling houses, and brothels, making it impossible for decent people with families to live in the village. John Sevak, who has not learned to accept defeat, tries other ways to accomplish his objective.

He approaches Rājā Mahendra Kumār, the chairman of the municipal committee, emphasizing the contribution industrialization makes to the economic development of the country. The Rājā promises to help him, a promise which involves him in the confrontation with Surdās. After some waverings of mind, which show his lack of principle, he acquires the land, and plans for the factory go ahead. Surdās mobilizes public opinion against this injustice. His peaceful struggle impresses Sophia, and she persuades Mr. Clark to cancel the acquisition. The Rājā takes it as a direct insult to his honor. He starts a propaganda campaign against Clark and waits in deputation on the governor of the province. He succeeds in his campaign: John Sevak gets the land again, and Clark is transferred, being appointed Resident in Udaipur State where Vinaya Singh is already engaged in social work.

However, once the factory is put up, more land is needed to build residential quarters for the workers. So the decision is taken to acquire Pāndépur itself. The villagers resist, and the police and army fire on the villagers. Surdās is gravely injured while trying to restrain the villagers. Rājā Mahendra Kumār undergoes a change of heart and begs Surdās's forgiveness. Surdās dies; a statue is put up in Pāndépur village as a mark of honor. The Rājā, despite his change of heart, is unable to stomach Surdās's glorification as a hero; he breaks the statue at night but is himself crushed under the broken part.

Surdās's contest with the authorities has its counterpart in the one with his own fellow villagers. He had, with great difficulty saved five hundred rupees to give shape to his dreams of developing his land. One night his cottage is set on fire and his money is stolen. The culprit is Bhairon, the mean and scheming liquor seller who suspects Surdās of having relations with his wife, Subhāgī. Surdās had given refuge and solace to her when she was beaten mercilessly by her drunken husband. Bhairon resented this and maligned and abused Surdās. But Subhāgī respected him as the only gentleman in the whole village. She brings him back the stolen money, but he refuses to accept it. In spite of Bhairon's hostile behavior Surdās bears no ill-will toward him and donates three hundred rupees for rebuilding his cottage after it has burned down. Surdās's generosity and friendliness finally win Bhairon's heart, and he becomes a friend and admirer.

The romantic interest of the story comes from the love affair between Vinaya and Sophia. Vinaya is doing social work in the princely state of Udaipur in Rajasthan. The state authorities, however, grow suspicious and put him in jail. Sophia rushes to Udaipur as soon as she gets this news. She tries her best to secure Vinaya's release and succeeds by enacting the drama of loving Mr. Clark who is the Resident here. Vinaya and Sophia come back to Benaras and are involved in the Pāndépur struggle. While trying to intervene in the confrontation between the police and the villagers, Vinaya shoots himself because the villagers question his integrity and refuse to listen to him. Sophia is heartbroken and commits suicide.

Rangabhumi has been regarded as a political and social novel written at the height of Prem Chand's enthusiasm for the freedom movement when a new era had begun in the political history of India with the advent of Gandhi and his introduction of nonviolent noncooperation. Surdās is seen as a Gandhian figure, an exponent and embodiment of the philosophy as well as the technique of nonviolent noncooperation. As such he appears on the scene holding "the key" to *swarāj* (self-rule, independence).[6] He symbolizes the victory of soul force over brute force, what one man can achieve when he possesses self-confidence and courage and is scrupulous about the means he employs to achieve his objective. This is all very true but undue emphasis on this aspect has had the unfortunate consequence of turning criticism of the novel into a debate on the merits of Gandhism as a political and social philosophy and on the degree of Prem Chand's commitment to it. As usual, other aspects of the novel like the cultural one have been ignored, and much less attention has been given to a discussion of the author's success or failure as an artist in embodying his vision.

Rangabhumi is, first, a fascinating account of the changing face of Indian society. Prem Chand is a superb social chronicler, and it is a delight to see how, with infinite patience and skill, he creates a real world in the novel. It is a chronicle of families: the Sevak family's evolution is traced over three generations, the Bharat Singh and the Ali family's over two. Their domestic life is portrayed in great detail, each little conflict having a larger significance and subserving the main themes of the novel. The character delineations bring out the ironies reflected in human nature and actions, the inconsistencies between professions and practice. The Sevak family has changed a great deal over three generations. Ishwar Sevak has imbued his capable son with his worldly wisdom but his grandchildren rebel against this unprincipled opportunism. Instead of making silly and shameful efforts to join the ranks of the ruling race, they take pride in their Indianness. The Rājās have also changed with the times, the extent of which can be realized by comparing those in British India with their kinsmen in the Indian States. The Dewān of Udaipur has no shame in describing himself and his cohorts as Negroes guarding the British harem and in mocking his own system of justice (213). Rājā Bharat Singh and Rājā Mahendra Kumār look like enlightened men as compared to these degenerate nincompoops. They are cultured and accomplished and have inculcated some sense of social obligation in their children. But their own personalities, as those of the Sevaks, have their inconsistencies. Mr. Sevak, in selling the idea of the cigarette factory, professes to contribute to the economic development of the country, but he has no hesitation in uprooting an entire community in seeking to achieve this development. Obviously, his professions are a fraud. Rājā Mahendra Kumār lives on the pretense of serving the people of the city when the men on his own estates from whom he collects lakhs of rupees every year suffer from neglect and injustice.

At the outset Prem Chand criticizes certain accepted ways of thinking in Indian society which illustrate the mental laziness of its members, their enslavement to superstition. One man is a *pāsī* ("liquor seller"), another is a *dhobī* ("washerman"), the third one is a *chamār* ("handler of dead animals"). A blind man is a *Surdās* (the name of a sixteenth-century saint-poet who was blind). This is the tyranny of the stereotype, a vicious habit of the mind which stops us from treating another man as an individual, a human being, and which, in its more virulent form, makes us coin despicable nicknames like "chink," "wog," "nigger," "kike," "goyim," "limey," or "wasp."

> In India blind people require neither a name nor an occupation. Surdās is their automatic name and begging their occupation. Their nature and attributes too are universally known—a particular aptitude for singing and performing, a particular love in the heart, particular involvement in spirituality and devotion. Outward vision blocked; inward vision open. (7)

One of Prem Chand's tasks in the novel is to prove the falsity of this categorization. Surdās is not just a stereotype: he is a person, a human being, superior in every respect to those who insult or patronize him. Whenever he displays uncommon wisdom, understanding, moral courage, or even physical strength, other people who are firmly persuaded of his inferiority to themselves feel surprised and attribute his virtues to the possession of some supernatural power. But Surdās is nothing more, Prem Chand with his intense humanism declares time and again, than a man.

The novel throws valuable light on Prem Chand's evolution as a social thinker. In *Premāshram* he still believed that the aristocracy and the educated elite were capable of providing leadership; in *Rangabhumi* he seems to have outgrown this belief. The aristocrats in the novel are all either weak or selfish creatures. Their idealism is only skin-deep, incapable of withstanding the slightest assault on their self-esteem. Rānī Jānhvī's is the most obvious example. Despite her immense wealth, she has given a highly puritanical upbringing to her son; but this is all for her personal glory or that of her class. As a consequence, he remains tied to her apron strings, showing little capacity for independent thinking and failing in every crisis. He is riled when in Udaipur he sees the rebel Vīrpāl

Singh leading the public demonstration. When a shot is fired at Sophia, without bothering to find out whether it came from an *agent provocateur*, he himself fires at Vīrpāl Singh. His last words, when he shoots himself during the confrontation between the villagers of Pāndépur and the police, are: "Do you want to see how the sons of aristocrats sacrifice themselves? Here you are—" (535). His sister Indu, the wife of Rājā Mahendra Kumār, is kind and gracious to Sophia so long as she can patronize her but becomes jealous and vindictive when she learns of Sophia's impending marriage with Clark. She has been posing as a champion of Surdās in the name of justice but when Sophia asks her to stop her husband from acquiring Surdās' land, her reply is: "A prince's prestige is much more important than trivial considerations of justice" (227). "Indu," her creator says, "could be benevolent—the feeling of mastership inheres in benevolence; she could not be just, for justice is based on equality" (246). What about Sophia? M. N. Gupta believes that she is only the female edition of Vinaya.[7] She is, however, in some ways, superior to him: Vinaya is merely an appendage of his mother; she has rejected her own. But though she is more courageous and high-minded than other members of her generation, when it comes to personal matters, she can be as small-minded as Indu. Prabhu Sevak, the young aesthete, is even more vacillating and confused. These are members of the younger generation; still their ideas and capacity for action are not much better than their seniors'. Indra Dutt is more vigorous but he is rather an exception. The idealism of the younger generation, Prem Chand tries to show, is mostly vague, airy, and muddled. It has no firm foundation and lacks the toughness of fiber which can be acquired only in the hard school of experience. The poor people of India cannot look to anyone to rescue them from oppression: they have to work out their own salvation.

It is important to understand this bitter truth because the new forces of capitalism are more intelligent, determined, and ruthless than those of the old feudalism. They can range the old feudalism on their side by offering it better opportunities to invest its money, while they are already the darlings of imperialism on account of their utter lack of principle and their willingness to do anything for it, howsoever dirty.

These generalizations about Prem Chand's social philosophy have to be made with reservations because they do not entirely square with the facts. M. N. Gupta is disappointed with him because his outlook is reactionary, totally under the spell of Gandhism. Surdās, according to Gupta, is representative of "that revolt against capitalism which is disorganized, sentimental and wears the varnish of religiosity."[8] Rāmvilās Sharmā answers this criticism with the counter question of whether there was any "organized revolution" going on anywhere which offered a choice to Prem Chand.[9] The answer is yes: a revolution had already taken place in Russia about five years earlier and Prem Chand knew about it. So far as India is concerned, whether preparations for a revolution were or were not going on, it was Prem Chand's business as a "sage" to say that such preparations ought to go on. But this line of thinking assumes that he believed in the necessity of revolution on class lines, which is extremely doubtful.[10] Surdās's chief antagonist in the novel appears to be not John Sevak but Rājā Mahendra Kumār, whose motives are not economic but egotistic. He is very much an Indian aristocrat of high caste and noble birth who is convinced of his inherent majesty in relation to an untouchable beggar. John Sevak, too, is more of an operator than an established industrialist. He does not come from the classes in Indian society which have been traditionally wealthy and which have played the leading role in industry—Pārsīs like the Tātās and Mārwarī *baniās* (members of the shopkeeping and moneylending caste) like the Birlās. Similarly, though Dr. Sharmā refers to them as *kisāns* (peasants or agriculturists),[11] the residents of Pāndépur village are not peasants. Pāndépur is not Lakhanpur, a real village; it is more like one of those agglomerations of cottages which spring up on the outskirts of large towns and in which the residents depend for their livelihood on the towns themselves. It is hardly fair, on the basis of the fight these people put up against the authorities, to generalize about feudalism, capitalism, and communism. It is not that Prem Chand did not understand the meaning of these terms, as M. N. Gupta patronizingly asserts;[12] there is documentary proof that he did. But he was doubtful about the applicability of these categories, evolved in the European context, to the Indian situation in which a high-caste communist looks down on his fellow communist because the latter is low-caste. It is good to remember that Prem Chand was a conservative and a humanist who believed in cooperation rather than in conflict and who was appalled by war and bloodshed. Sharmā has argued that he was not opposed to industrialization, whereas those who see him as a committed Gandhian claim that he was. The question can be easily answered by examining his philosophy of life and his moral outlook.

Prem Chand was an advocate of a life of simple living and high thinking, for the nation as for the individual. He believed that India is an agricultural country and that agriculture should receive the main emphasis in any scheme of economic development. He was opposed to large-scale industrialization because of the evils that follow in its wake, of which he gives a practical demonstration in this novel. Surdās' views about the cigarette factory are thus a faithful echo of Prem Chand's own. But he did believe in small-scale industry—of the kind "which the peasants could pursue in their leisure time sitting at home."[13] Obviously, Prem Chand's vision of a free India did not include the establishment of a modern and powerful state, with its flourishing network of foreign trade, its extensive armed forces, and a sophisticated armaments industry.

Though the social and economic issues are important, *Rangabhumi* is primarily a political novel, written at a time when Prem Chand's mind was occupied with the nature and course of India's struggle for freedom. Pāndépur is a symbolic representation of India, a microcosm of the great macrocosm which includes poor people of different castes and creeds (Tāhir Ali's wife Kulsum also takes shelter there after his imprisonment). The cigarette factory represents the encroachment of an alien and more aggressive rule and culture, an encroachment which becomes possible because of disunity among residents of the village. The chief agent in this encroachment is John Sevak, the Christian convert who, in the unprincipled pursuit of his self-interest, seeks the assistance of the foreign ruler. He is aided in his designs by Rājā Mahendra Kumār, typifying the Indian aristocrats who welcomed the British to ensure their own future but who were reduced to complete impotence by their new masters. Sophia represents the Europeans who in spite of their ties with the ruling race had, like Mrs. Besant, chosen to identify themselves with the cause of Indian independence, moved by a sense of justice but also by admiration for India's great culture. (The parallel between Sophia and Mrs. Besant is not exact.) Surdās is Indian nationalism, his frailness indicative of the economic and military weakness of India as compared to the overpowering strength of the *Rāj*. The only way to prevail against such overwhelming power is through moral strength, the way suggested by Mahātmā Gandhi. *Satyāgraha* is literally "insistence on truth," the natural order of things, and refusal to compromise with anyone who, subverting this natural order, demands submission to an artificial scheme of things through force or the threat of force. The atural order, which is fundamentally moral, assures to every na-on, as it does to every man, the right to life, liberty, and the pur-iit of happiness. Any authority which, sheltering itself behind law, eeks to deprive men of these basic freedoms is itself violating igher laws and has thus no right to demand compliance. Refusal to ooperate with it is a right as well as a duty. When Indra Dutt tries convince Surdās that his hut is being acquired not forcibly but gally, the latter questions the validity of this man-made law in lation to a higher law, the law of *dharma*, of righteousness, "the nly law I recognize and accept" (510). Surdās's thesis is a cogent xposition of Gandhi's philosophy of noncooperation, or the moral round on which Indian nationalism had taken its stand.

But when it comes to his larger philosophy of life—his conception f the universe as the playground of the creator, and of cultivating a oical indifference to victory and defeat—he is the beneficiary of e great Indian religious tradition. The title of the novel comes robably from one of the poems of a medieval Hindi saint-poet hich, translated from Hindi, reads as follows:

> You are a wonderful puppet-master, O, My Lord;
> Like a stage you have made this creation, with
> the curtain of *Māyā;*
> You make man dance in various ways. . . .

he doctrine of selfless action both Gandhi and Prem Chand learn-d from the *Bhāgwadgītā.*[14] It is the kind of action which does not bind," does not entangle us deeper in the cycle of birth and ebirth thereby becoming an obstacle in the way of deliverance. However, neither the Gītā nor any other of the scriptures, as far as I now, says that man should take life as a sport, as Surdās repeatedly iggests and as Prem Chand himself advised his friend Nigam to do his letter of 23 April 1923 (*Chitthī-Patrī*, I, 133 - 34). The idea of stoical indifference to victory and defeat, loss and gain which ves us from elation and depression, from nursing grudges which itiate our moral being, is borrowed from Indian religious literature, ut the idea of treating life as a sport is, I think, Prem Chand's own, nd he should be given full credit for this exciting concept.

Surdās' success and failure should be viewed within this frame of ference. "We suffer defeat," Prem Chand wrote in 1933, "when e fall from the ideal of humility, when we begin cursing and abus-g, when, gripped by a feeling of retaliation . . . we attack"

(*Vividh Prasang*, II, 65). Success and failure are thus, in the spirit the true *satyāgrahī*, conceived in moral terms. And from this poi of view, Surdās is greater in his defeat than his oppressors in the victory. But, even on the purely mundane level, Surdās did not e tirely fail. "There was a dinner in the evening in which high-cas Hindus and untouchables were eating together. This was Surdā greatest triumph" (574). By referring to the communal dinner Surdās' greatest triumph, Prem Chand is trying to restore our sen of perspective. The great struggle of Surdās' life is not with the ric and powerful but with his own people. When fighting against th former he never for a moment loses his self-confidence and aplom when fighting against his own ignorant and opinionated neighbor he cries and weeps and, Job-like, curses the hour in which he w born. His real cross is not the plot of land or the hut but Subhāg While sheltering her from the tyranny of her husband Bhairon an the calumny of the entire village, his house is set on fire and he ostracized, insulted, and abused. But he stands by his *dharm* ("ideal proper conduct" as Tagore translates the word), firm an steadfast like a rock. "A man who turns his back on *dharma* for fe of getting a bad name is no man," he says (130). When he is stan ing by Subhāgī, Surdās is not merely a Gandhian, but Gand himself, for Subhāgī, at the symbolic level, is oppressed humanit particularly the untouchable class in India. Nothing broug Gandhi in such bitter conflict with the prestigious and powerf among his countrymen as his championship of the cause of th *harijans* ("Children of God," the name given to the Untouchabl by Gandhi). But how could the Indians fight against British i justice and claim their rights when they continued to den justice—their basic rights as human beings—to their own kith an kin?

Surdās' struggle for the land is not for the sacred principle private property but for the inalienable right of every man to be th master of his own destiny. The struggle between him and th bigwigs is a struggle between two philosophies of life—th philosophy of self-interest and the philosophy which believes th the individual's own good is bound up with the good of the societ to which he belongs. This is the same theme which Prem Chan had taken up in *Premāshram* and, as in the earlier novel, moder civilization is castigated as the great culprit. John Sevak's lineag should be traced to Gyān Shankar; so also that of Māhir Ali and, i a small way, that of Surdās' nephew Mithvā. Māhir Ali, a product ıodern education, refuses to recognize the children of his elder rother who had made himself a pauper while trying to get him an English" education. Surdās represents the Indian cultural tradiion, but even the Rājās come out better than that unwavering otary of self-interest, John Sevak. And the ironies are extremely isturbing. The blind beggar Surdās, an untouchable, is more truly hivalrous in his firm adherence to Subhāgī than all the high-born nd boastful Rājput princes, just as he is more truly religious than he agents of religion like Nāyak Rām, Devagiri, etc.

Rangabhumi is, in spite of its weaknesses—a slightly loose contruction and the authorial commentary which insists on explaining very pattern of behavior in general terms—a great novel and ilustrates the steady evolution of Prem Chand's art. Whether or not he inspiration originally came from George Eliot's *Silas Marner*, vhich Prem Chand had adapted in Hindi a few years earlier, it was bold step to make a blind beggar the hero of an ambitious novel. 'rem Chand is successful in portraying Surdās not only as a heroic igure[15] but also as "a positively good man," a difficult task in ficion as even a master like Dostoevski realized.[16] Prem Chand's viion here is tragic, inclining him to a more willing acceptance of eality and avoidance of shortcuts to happiness like the establishnent of Abodes of Love.

III Metamorphosis: *God and Mammon*

Kāyākalp (Metamorphosis) is not the story of one but many netamorphoses, in the flesh as well as in the spirit. The most conpicuous of these is that of Rānī Devapriyā and Rājkumār Inlravikram Singh (Mahendra). The Rānī is an aging aristocrat levoted to a life of self-indulgence, a votary of Cupid whose most herished wish is to gain her former youth and beauty. This wish is ulfilled by the Rājkumār who is a reincarnation of her husband. He s involved in the recurring cycle of birth because of his ungratified passion for the Rānī. His contact with a religious mystic in Tibet, who claimed to have been Darwin in his previous life but is now a student of the science of the spirit, has given him the ability to recall incidents from his former life. Recognizing Devapriyā the moment he sees her, he invites her to come to the mountains with him. Regaining her lost youth, she follows him. Mahendra shows her his scientific laboratories and takes her on a plane ride. However, as soon as he reaches out to make love to her, the plane begins to fall and finally crashes. Mahendra is dead but Devapriyā survives. Sh goes back to her husband's estates at Harshpur.

The second transformation is that of Chakradhar, the hero of th tale. He is the son of Munshī Vajradhar, a retired revenue offici who is a strange mixture of servility and generosity, of worldline and detachment. Chakradhar is a gifted young man, intelligen well-educated, and extremely idealistic. While his father is con tantly prodding him to take up a job and make some money, he ha decided to devote himself to the service of the people. To assist h aged father, he accepts part-time work coaching Manoramā, th thirteen-year-old daughter of Thākur Harisevak Singh, the chie minister of Jagdishpur State. Manoramā is a bright, impulsive, an brave girl. Her intense admiration for her high-minded tutor turn into love. The two lovers, however, keep their passion under stric control and take other partners. Manoramā becomes the fourth wif of Rājā Vishāl Singh, while Chakradhar marries Ahilyā, giving proc of his high-mindedness, for she had been kidnapped during th Hindu-Muslim riots in Agra, and most Hindus considered he "polluted." His own parents do not take the food prepared by he This annoys Chakradhar into leaving their home in Benaras an moving to Allahabad, where he devotes himself to social work. Th couple's five-year stay in Allahabad has been fruitful and happy an they are blessed with a son, Shankhdhar.

There is a sudden change in this even tenor of life, paving th way for several metamorphoses. Manoramā is gravely ill i Jagdishpur and Chakradhar, informed of the illness, immediatel goes there with Ahilyā. Manoramā regains her health as soon as sh sees him. Also, Rājā Vishāl Singh recognizes Ahilyā as his daughte who had been lost at the Kumbh Fair about twenty years ago. Th Rājā, who in spite of his six marriages has no issue, is mad with jo for he has found not only a daughter and a very worthy son-in-la but also a grandson and heir. Wealth and status, however, d strange things to these nice people. Ahilyā becomes a slave to lu ury and shows no enthusiasm when her husband wishes to return t his life of social service. But Chakradhar is changed too. Once whe some villagers decline to salvage his car from a ravine in the middl of the night, he hits and injures one of them, fatally, as it turns ou later. The incident makes him aware of the corrupting influence o power and money and, one night when everyone is asleep, he slip out from the Rājā's palace to resume his career of social service.

Seven years have elapsed. Shankhdhar, now an intense an

arnest lad of thirteen, starts making pressing inquiries about his ather and, finding no satisfaction, sets out in search of him. After ive years' ceaseless efforts, he does succeed in finding him. As they re living together, news of his mother's illness obliges him to eturn to Jagdishpur. But when the train passes through Harshpur, inding the surroundings familiar, he gets off. Shankhdhar is really Mahendra, Devapriyā's husband, in a third incarnation. She is still eigning here, now known as Kamlā. Shankhdhar, regaining his nemory of former lives, restores her to youth, marries her, and akes her to Jagdishpur. The same story is repeated: one day, eaching out to make love to her he drops dead. The shock kills 'ishāl Singh too. Devapriyā (now Kamlā) again starts ruling in agdishpur but she is now a metamorphosed Kamlā, devoted to a ife of austerity and service. Chakradhar comes back to Jagdishpur nly to discover that his son is dead and his wife is dying. After seeng Manoramā, he departs. But his soul cannot find peace in separaion from her. He takes to keeping birds and, one day, leaves two irds in separate cages at Manoramā's palace.

The realistic part of the novel portrays political life in the nidtwenties when the country was riven by Hindu-Muslim riots. 'ashodā Nandan and Khwājā Mahmood are the leaders of the opposing factions which indulge in killing each other. The riots occur wice. Chakradhar distinguishes himself in the earlier ones, stoping a bloody outbreak by putting his own life at stake. The mischief is already done in the later ones before he appears. Yashodā Nandan is murdered and Ahilyā is abducted by the Khwājā's own on, whom she kills to protect her honor. The murder of his close riend Yashodā Nandan opens the Khwājā's eyes. He realizes the rrant folly of communalism and experiences a metamorphosis.

Another aspect of sociopolitical life is presented in the conflict between the peasants of Jagdishpur and their landlord Rājā Vishāl Singh. The Rājā, who at one time held enlightened views, becomes arrogant and tyrannical as soon as he gets power. He calls in the British soliders when the *chamārs* who have been commandeered to work at his "coronation" refuse to do so because they have been given no food for a week. The soldiers resort to firing, killing many of them and injuring Chakradhar, who is acting as their leader. In spite of his commendable role in restraining them and in saving the British officers from the wrath of the public, he is arrested and sent o prison. His sentence is reduced and release secured through the strenuous efforts of Rānī Manoramā.

Kāyākalp was the first novel to be written originally in Hindi. Having completed *Rangabhumi* on 1 April 1924, Prem Chand started work on *Kāyākalp* on the tenth of the same month. It was completed some time early in 1926 and published by July of the same year.[17] Most critics, put off by Prem Chand's use of the supernatural, dismiss it as a failure. Goyankā is probably the only critic who makes a sincere effort to understand the novel. He rejects the view that there are two stories in it existing independently of each other, and insists on its thematic unity, mental transformation being the main theme and physical transformation the subsidiary one. The author is trying to show that wealth is the root cause of all evil, self-indulgence and love of power being its natural accompaniments. Goyankā distinguishes between the two kinds of metamorphoses presented in the novel, both illustrated by Devapriyā's story. Her restoration to youth and beauty is really no metamorphosis; the real and true one is that of her mind which she experiences after Shankhdhar's death.

This analysis is very perceptive, though it does not explain the significance of the miraculous element in the novel, its place in the total structure. Emphasis on thematic unity is sound. Metamorphosis, however, is not only of two kinds but also of two types—the negative and the positive. The positive one is experienced by Khwājā Mahmood after his friend Yashodā Nandan's murder during the communal riots, by Chakradhar after the incident with Dhannā Singh, and by Devapriyā following Shankhdhar's death. The negative one brought about by wealth, power, or passion is illustrated by the stories of Rājā Vishāl Singh, Ahilyā, Chakradhar, and, in a horrifying way, by that of Mahendra Shankhdhar. The brief outline of the plot prepared by the author demonstrates that the negative one was more central to his moral purpose: "Ideas: Trials and troubles mold the human character; they make heroes of men; power and authority is the curse of humanity; even the highest fall a victim to power and lose their character. Chakradhar rose morally while struggling for existence; his fall began when he came to power."[18]

The theme is taken up early in the novel itself (98). Manoramā writes an essay on "The Blessings of Wealth and Power," which, according to her, lie in triumph over the ravages of time, over public opinion, and even over the soul. Chakradhar, her tutor, is surprised and shocked to see such "obscene thoughts" finding a place in her mind. Manoramā expresses her regrets, promising never to write an ssay like this again. But Chakradhar insists on enlightening and onvincing her:

t is not a matter of writing. Such thoughts ought not even to enter your ıind. We triumph over the ravages of time through good name, sacrifice, nd dedication. Only altruism confers immortality. Triumph over the avages of time does not mean that we should indulge in pleasure resorting ɔ artificial means, should dream of youth in old age and betray our soul. 'riumph over public opinion means earning the esteem of the people hrough our noble thoughts and noble deeds. Triumph over the soul does ot mean shamelessness and self-indulgence but the subduing of desires nd checking of our evil tendencies. (98 - 99)

'he flaw in Manoramā's thesis lay not in its lack of realism but ather in its stark realism, its brutality as fact. "Factual reality," says ;hakradhar, "is the most frightening thing in the world: the world ould become a hell if we were to accept the fact as our ideal" (99). lso, among the "blessings" of wealth and power is one which she ad neglected to mention—forgetting our earlier selves, what we ere before. Chakradhar's sarcasm has an air of foreboding. The ony lies in the circumstance that though Manoramā apologizes for er opinions she does not abandon them, and that Chakradhar, with ll his oracular wisdom, will not be immune to the corrupting effect f power. She will be attracted by wealth and dominion, acting no oubt in the honest belief that she could use them for good.

Thus while the main theme of *Kāyākalp* is the degrading inuence of wealth, power, and passion, there are two subsidiary ones ıinistering to the main theme. The first one, as we have already een, unfolds in the form of a debate between Manoramā and ;hakradhar on two ways of doing good, of serving the people—one hrough accession to wealth and power; the other through spurning hese and leading a life of austerity identifying oneself with the people. It is likely that Prem Chand was through this debate dramatizng the controversy which had raged in the Indian National ;ongress on the desirability of entering the legislatures, causing a plit and leading to the formation of the Swarāj Party under the eadership of Motīlāl Nehru and C. R. Dās.[19] His own preference is lear. Like Gandhi he is against "Council-entry" and believes that he Congress ought to concentrate on serving the people. Accession o power will alienate it from the masses, for even the wisest and the nost well-intentioned (Chakradhar and Vishāl Singh) cannot escape he corruption wrought by power.

The second subtheme too bolsters the main one. Dazzled by the triumphs of science and technology, modern man adopts a cavalier attitude to the findings of the science of the spirit. But the latter are no less valid; in fact, their validity is greater so far as the moral and spiritual welfare of man is concerned. Mahendra, after having spent seven years in the West trying to discover the essence of life, meets a Tibetan monk in a laboratory in Berlin. The monk points out the futility of seeking spiritual knowledge in material-empirical knowledge and advises him to go to Tibet in the East. He takes the advice and meets there the sage who in his previous life had been Darwin, the great scientist. Obviously, biological science had failed to enlighten him, so he has studied and mastered the science of the spirit. His preeminence in both fields places him in a unique position to make a comparative evaluation. He imparts both kinds of knowledge to Mahendra, but the pupil is so impressed by the physical that he ignores the spiritual. He acquires powers of various kinds but lacks the wisdom to use them properly. That is why he is involved in the cycle of birth and death.

Kāyākalp is not a realistic novel. Prem Chand's deep preoccupation with the moral problem makes it more of a parable, and we can appreciate it only by looking at his fictional world at the two levels delineated by J. R. R. Tolkien—our primary world of daily fact and the "secondary world" of fantasy which, while possessing an "internal consistency," has also "strangeness and wonder" arising from its "freedom from the domination of observed fact."[20] As in the novels of Iris Murdoch, Prem Chand's fictional strategy involves a mythic universe in which mystery suggests the existence of a higher order beyond our material-empirical notions of reality. Recourse to this universe becomes necessary because he wants to talk about spiritual-psychic forces that cannot be portrayed in realistic fiction but which constitute the very basis of the moral world.[21]

Prem Chand's mythic universe, recognizing the supremacy of spiritual values, makes an uncompromising division between the realms of God and Mammon, with no middle ground between them. His deep puritanism is seen in the story of Ahilyā. Though her sin is only venial, it invites a harsh punishment. Vishāl Singh meets the same fate, the death of Shankhdhar falling like a thunderbolt on him. It is clear that Prem Chand's stern and inexorable Law brooks no indulgence, knows no forgiveness. For if wealth and power are the agents of Mammon and pursuing them is bad for the soul, passion—the desire for physical contact with woman, what the 'orld calls sex—is lethal. Devapriyā and Mahendra commit this ıortal sin and therefore suffer tortures of unfulfilled desire and epeated birth and death, the cycle being broken by Devapriyā only 'hen she realizes her mistake and devotes herself to a life of austeri- y and service.

The novel, however, operates on another plane—our primary 'orld of daily fact, and here it has a documentary value. The olitical situation in the country immediately before and during the ears Prem Chand was working on the novel was extremely depress- ıg. The noncooperation movement started by Gandhi early in 1921 ad to be suspended on 12 February 1922 because it was turning in- reasingly violent. Twenty-one policemen were murdered by a iolent mob on 4 February 1922 at Chaurī Chaurā village in ;orakhpur district, Uttar Pradesh, not far from the place where 'rem Chand used to live a few years ago. His dismay at this turn of vents is reflected both in *Rangabhumi* and *Kāyākalp*. The leading haracters in these novels—Vinaya, Surdās, and Chakradhar—risk ıeir lives trying to control angry mobs bent on violence. But he was articularly distressed by the Hindu-Muslim riots which had shown dramatic increase during these years. Animosity between the two ommunities had intensified with the starting of the *shuddhi* 'purification") movement by the Ārya Samāj in 1924, sanctioning ɔr the first time reconversion to Hinduism of those Hindus who ad been converted to Islam. Since most of the Indian Muslims /ere originally Hindus, the movement created alarm among the 1uslims.[22] Prem Chand had expressed his strong disapproval of this ıovement in his essay "Dearth of Humanity" published in the *amānā* for February 1924 *(Vividh Prasang,* II, 351 - 57). In *āyākalp* he blames the leaders of both communities who were in- iting their followers and were thus making human beings behave ke savage beasts. Through the story of Ahilyā and the treatment he gets from Chakradhar's parents he ridicules the pretensions of he Hindus. They were out to reconvert those who had embraced slam, but no respectable man among them was prepared to marry a irl who had been abducted by the Muslims. Munshī Vajradhar in is conventional wisdom is the spokesman of respectable Hinduism, nd in his wife Nirmalā's rebuke to him when he objects to his son's ıarriage to Ahilyā we can detect the accents of Prem Chand's own oice: "Your *dharma* ["honour"] does not suffer when you accept ribes; your face is not blackened when you drink like a fish; you do ıot commit a sin when you build edifices of lies. But if the boy comes to the rescue of an orphan girl, then you are disgraced in th public eye" (211).

Portions of the novel which deal with the communal riots in Agr are a faithful portrayal of the contemporary situation, though th dramatic metamorphosis of Khwājā Mahmood and the triumphs c Chakradhar are too good to be true. Chakradhar is in the line o Prem Chand's earnest and high-minded young heroes who projec an ideal. These are the kind of young men who will bring freedor to the country and be the pioneers in establishing a new social orde based on justice and equality. Unfortunately they never come t life, though Chakradhar is more real than Prem Shankar and Vinay Singh. Prem Chand portrays his character with greater sophistica tion but does not fully suceed in making him a living person. Bu Manoramā is more real and so is Longī. However, the most aliv and entertaining character in the novel is Munshī Vajradhar. Th old man—boastful, cringing, and servile but humane, generou and large-hearted—is a relic of the past, embodying the strengths a well as weaknesses of the old order.

The novel is also a story of love—the Platonic and selfless love c Manorama for Chakradhar, which the author treats with respec and portrays with delicacy. Every step that Manoramā takes in he life is with the sole object of pleasing or helping her noble tutor an idol. Restless to know about his reaction to her marriage with Vish Singh, she is pleased and relieved when Chakradhar, on his releas from prison, tells her that he was "both sad and angry" at the new (205). In the end he does appreciate her love. Like her he become fond of birds and presents a few to Manoramā. The two birds i cages he leaves with the gardener symbolize these two star-crosse lovers. They have to stay in separate cages, bound as they are b their former loyalties and the conventions of the world. It is als these constraints which prevent Chakradhar from seeing Manoram and presenting the birds to her in person.

Kāyākalp, with all the author's spirit of experimentation an boldness of conception, is a dissatisfying work, in no way com parable to *Seva-Sadan*, *Premashram*, or *Rangabhumi*. The mai cause of its ruin is Prem Chand's obsessive and stern moralism There is less of enactment and more of comment, and the frequen authorial intrusions become tiresome and irritating. The sentimen tality is almost sickening. The usual regimen of falling and crying a others' feet is repeated about a dozen times. Chakradhar is s overwhelmed by Ahilyā's bravery in killing her assaulter that h 'ishes to see the dagger she had used (214). Shankhdhar's search or his father is overdone. When he finally finds him and is lying in is lap, the author exclaims: "O denizens of the sky, why don't you nake a rain of flowers!" (321). The narrative does not flow in a nooth and natural manner; episodes and incidents are contrived to rove a point; for instance, Chakradhar's encounter with the bull 'hen he is riding in his car and then the brush with the villagers 256 - 57).

Madan Gopāl has tried to explain the weakness of the novel by eferring to the financial worry and strain Prem Chand was experiencing during these years, consequent on the establishment of he press.[23] Undoubtedly this was a troubled period in his life. A aughter born on 8 March 1924 had passed away on 7 June, plunging the family in gloom and sickness. His own health was very bad. n addition to the chronic stomach ailment from which he suffered, alf of his right heel had to be lopped off in August 1925 because of festering wound caused by a nail in his sandal.[24] But there is also ailure of inspiration, possibly owing to exhaustion after writing hree major novels. Prem Chand seems to be in a highly introspective and self-conscious mood. Chakradhar's predicament seems to e his own—whether he should follow the path of duty by refusing o compromise with the forces of injustice and tyranny, suffering overty and neglect, or, becoming worldly-wise like Chakradhar's ather, seek prosperity and success. He had already made his choice y resigning from government service but the strain was still there. *āyākalp* is an exercise in vindication of this choice; hence its stern nd persistent moralism. It is also very likely, I think, that he was ed to this experiment in fantasy by the example of Anatole France 'hose *Thais* he was rendering into Hindi at the same time as he was 'orking on this novel. France's moralism he had inbibed, but the ervasive and pleasant irony of his conception he had missed completely.

CHAPTER 6

Novels of the Third Phase, 1926 - 28

I Nirmalā: *the Stranded Voyager*

NIRMALĀ is the tragic story of a young girl who is married to a man more than twice her own age. Nirmalā is engaged to a young man of good family but, a few days before the wedding, her father, a well-to-do lawyer, is murdered by an ex-convict. The groom's father cancels the marriage because now, after the death of the lawyer, he will not get a handsome dowry. Nirmalā's widowed mother marries her to Munshī Totā Rām because he does not demand a dowry. Though Nirmalā is barely fifteen, Totā Rām is about forty, and looks older. He has also three sons by his first marriage—Mansā Rām, the eldest, is sixteen, Jiyā Rām is about eleven, and Siyā Rām is seven. His fifty-year-old widowed sister also resides with him.

Totā Rām, a balding lawyer of indifferent health, tries to please his young and beautiful wife, using every resource mentioned in the marriage manuals, but receives no response. Nirmalā, as a dutiful Hindu wife, is prepared to do everything for her venerable husband except returning his love. She is nice to her stepsons and develops a liking for Mansā Rām, an extremely intelligent, sensitive, and decent boy of her own age. She begins taking English lessons from him. This arouses suspicion in the mind of Munshī Totā Rām who starts being nasty to the boy and tries to send him to the school hostel to keep him away from his youthful wife. Mansā is deeply hurt by his father's rude behavior. He insists on joining the hostel himself but his health deteriorates rapidly when he divines the real cause of the father's hostility. He becomes critically ill and has to be moved to hospital where he slips into a state of delirium. Nirmalā, to allay her husband's suspicions, assumes a posture of indifference to Mansā's fate and even allows Totā Rām to make love to her. But 'hen she learns that the boy's condition is critical and that the only 'ay to save him is through transfusion of a young person's blood, ıe discards all caution and rushes to Mansā's bedside in the ospital to offer her own blood. Mansā falls at her feet and, to es- ablish her innocence in her husband's eyes, tells her that he had lways looked upon her as his mother and that his fondest wish was) be born out of her loins. While Nirmalā's blood is still being umped out, Mansā breathes his last.

Nirmalā finds a friend in Sudhā, wife of the doctor who had been 'eating Mansā. She tells Sudhā the story of her life; how her im- ending marriage to a young man could not materialize owing to er father's death and her mother's inability to give a big dowry. udhā discovers that the young man in question was no other than er own worthy husband, Dr. Sinhā. As a restitution for the wrong one by him and his family to Nirmalā, Dr. Sinhā persuades his arents to accept her younger sister Krishnā as a bride for his ounger brother, without asking for a dowry. Nirmalā, when she earns the facts, is overwhelmed with gratitude.

She is now the mother of a small girl who closely resembles Man- ā and is taken to be his incarnation. But things with Nirmalā's hus- and are not going well. His house has already been put up for auc- ion and his legal practice is steadily declining. The second boy falls ı with bad company, becoming rude and insulting to his father vhom he accuses of having poisoned Mansā. One night he steals he casket containing all of Nirmalā's ornaments. She had seen him eaving her room at night but when the theft is detected the next ay she does not disclose this information for fear of being accused f stepmotherly behavior. Munshījī reports the theft to the police, ut when the police identify his own son as the criminal he gets ttery and blames Nirmalā for placing him in a desperate situation. 3y the time he hushes the matter up through bribing the police in- pector, Jiyā has already disappeared and never shows up again.

The theft of her ornaments brings about a radical change in Nir- nalā's nature. Anxiety for her own future—but, even more, her laughter's—makes her stingy, mean, and callous. Frustrated by her ehavior, Siyā Rām, the youngest boy, vanishes with a *sādhu* wandering ascetic or monk). Totā Rām, a broken man estranged rom Nirmalā, goes out in search of him. Nirmalā's difficulties are, owever, not yet over. Dr. Sinhā, excited by her beauty, makes ad- 'ances to her. She rebuffs him, but when Sudhā comes to know of he incident, she is furious with her husband and castigates him. He dies all of a sudden. Nirmalā too falls ill and dies. As her dead bod is about to be carried away for cremation and the question is bein asked as to who would perform the last rites, an old wayfarer with small bundle shows up who turns out to be Munshī Totā Rām.

Nirmalā was serialized in the women's magazine *Chānd* (Th Moon) between November 1925 and November 1926. Critics hav offered different explanations for Prem Chand's choice of theme Madan Gopāl thinks that *Nirmalā* "is the abridged version of som novel which Prem Chand had written in early life when theme such as these [that is, of a social nature] had moved him."[1] Rāmvilā Sharmā suggests that he took to more purely social themes becaus he was disillusioned with the noncooperation movement.[2]

Nirmalā is neither an early work nor a product of Prem Chānd' disillusionment with the noncooperation movement, and Goyankā i right to disagree with both these explanations. "The greatest mis fortune that has happened to *Nirmalā*," he believes, "is that critic have evaluated it fixing the time of its composition three-four year earlier than the actual date of its publication."[3] Also, Prem Chand' writing of *Karmabhumi* proves that he did not consider the non cooperation movement a failure. These opinions show a lack of un derstanding of Prem Chand's outlook and purpose. Social reform t him was not something different from the freedom movement bu rather an essential and inseparable part of the struggle. The choic of a social theme was, I think, partly dictated by the need of writin something which might be suitable for a woman's magazine, a com pulsion arising from his increased popularity. But the loss o momentum and direction by the freedom movement also perhap contributed to the choice.

Nirmalā is an excellent work, demonstrating the progressiv evolution of Prem Chand's art as a novelist. He shows greater ski in narration, plot construction, and character portrayal, achieving degree of concentration not seen in any previous novel. The stor proceeds at a faster pace, events are narrated in a more matter-of fact way. Instead of lingering over them, Prem Chand spends mor time on psychological analysis, unraveling the stream of th characters' consciousness. It is really a psychological novel in whic most of the action takes place in the minds of the characters. Th news of her impending marriage transforms a young, immature gir of fifteen into a "serious, solitude-loving, and bashful" woman (25) A strange atmosphere of preternatural mystery, of an impendin tragedy, pervades the novel. As the elaborate preparations for he marriage go on, Nirmalā is haunted by an unknown, indefinabl ear: "Nobody knows what will happen." At night she dreams that he is stranded on the bank of an overflowing river and darkness is escending. A boat appears and Nirmalā is cheered up, but as soon s she tries to board it the sailor tells her that there is no room for er. She is desperate; a small skiff is seen, battered and leaky, vithout sail, without oars or rudder. The sailor offers her a place; he hesitates but, having no other resource, accepts the offer. Very oon the skiff is full of water and about to sink. Nirmalā shouts for elp, but suddenly the dream is over and she wakes up. The dream ; a presentiment: the strong and sturdy boat which refuses to ccept Nirmalā is the young man who will refuse to marry her; the eaking and battered skiff is her future husband, Munshī Totā Rām.

There must be something drastically wrong with a society in hich a woman is like a stranded voyager who must ever implore oatmen to take her across the foaming river of life. Prem Chand's riticism in the novel is directed not simply at the custom of dowry vhich involves estimable young girls in unequal marriages but at he totally subservient position of women in a society controlled by nales. The dowry system is bad enough. It makes the birth of a emale child a source of worry and anxiety. Nirmalā's nature is niraculously transformed after the birth of her daughter and the heft of her ornaments. The same Nirmalā who was soft-spoken, ind, and generous now becomes tart-tongued, hard, and stingy. he has to save for her daughter's dowry so that the girl is not hrown away into the lap of a decaying old man like her own husand. The dependent condition of women obliges their own nothers to mete out stepmotherly treatment to them. Nirmalā's nother Kalyānī could have married her to a decent young man if he had spent one thousand rupees on her dowry, but she was more oncerned about the future of her young sons: "Her sons were far earer to her than her daughters. Boys are the bullocks who carry he plough; they are entitled to hay and oilcakes. The cows should et the leftovers after the former are fed" (56). Kalyānī is not being ncommonly callous; she is acting just as any other woman in her osition would have done.

Totā Rām is no villain either. He is the follower of a system, his nly fault being that he is too conventional and thinks and behaves xactly like other members of his society:

haven't done anything outlandish [he says to himself]. All men and vomen marry. Their lives pass happily. It is the desire for happiness which eads us to marry. Hundreds of people in the neighborhood have married a

> second, third, fourth, even a seventh time and they are much older than I am. . . . My father himself had married when he was fifty-five and he was not less than sixty at the time of my birth. (118)

Totā Rām, in marrying a woman much younger than himself, was merely following tradition; the fault therefore was more of the society which saw nothing wrong in such marriages.

Nirmalā is not simply a study of the pitiable lot of women but also of dependent children, as Rāmvilās Sharmā points out.[4] Like Samuel Butler in *The Way of All Flesh,* Prem Chand exposes the tyranny of the father. Totā Rām thinks that he has the right to order his sons about because he supports them. The root of all evil, Prem Chand suggests, is the rampant spirit of commercialism which has vitiated all human relationships. In a society based on money, marriage is not a union of two human beings joined in love and friendship but a transaction in which the party of the male, being the stronger of the two, tries to strike the best bargain. Prem Chand is comparatively lenient to the older generation—Bābu Bhāl Chandra Sinhā is portrayed as a figure of broad comedy—but he is unsparing to the younger one. Sudhā is acting as the author's surrogate when she upbraids her husband for his refusal to marry Nirmalā after her father's death.

Prem Chand's social outlook has, however, its limitations. He does not suggest that Totā Rām should have married a widow his own age, or that marriage should be based on the free choice of boys and girls, or that Nirmalā could marry again after Totā Rām's death had she survived him. His commitment is wholly to the orthodox Hindu ideal which enjoins that the wife should be devoted to the husband whatever the odds against her. Of course he demands equal loyalty from the husband, as is evident from Sudhā's incredible remark that widowhood is not worse than marriage to a disloyal husband (205).

There is a new realism in the portrayal of character in this novel. Prem Chand recognizes the importance of sex, and Nirmalā is different from his sexless heroines like Virjan, Sophia, and Manoramā. We are pleasantly surprised by Nirmalā's frank admission to her sister Krishnā in regard to Mansā that had his intentions been immodest, she would have gone all out to accommodate him (139).

Nirmalā is a very human, pathetic, and touching story, not only of Nirmalā but also of Totā Rām, which, raising it above social criticism, makes it a tale of man's helplessness in the face of forces beyond his control. The staggering series of deaths in the novel, highly unnatural at the purely realistic level, seem to be designed to confirm this impression. The social system itself, which hems us in on all sides and makes us act stupidly, becomes an instrument of these mysterious forces. Prem Chand's greatest success lies in retaining artistic control by restraining his impulse to preach and checking himself from being swept away by his usual emotionalism which often slides into sentimentalism. It is a measure of this control that the customary falling at the feet occurs only once in the novel and, that too, when it seems most appropriate and natural.

II The Vow: *Man and Woman*

There is a great deal of confusion in the minds of scholars on the relationship between the novels *Premā* and *Pratigyā* (The Vow), the former written before 1905 and published about 1907, the latter serialized in *Chānd* from January to November 1927 and put out in book form in 1929. Goyankā has cleared away most of the confusion by pointing out that *Premā* and *Pratigyā* are two separate works.[5] The latter is in every aspect infinitely superior to the former, the only things common between the two being the basic theme, the principal characters, and the broad framework of the story.

In *Pratigyā* the names of the characters remain the same but the plot has undergone a radical change. Amrit Rāi does refuse to marry Premā because of his vow to marry a widow. But he marries neither Purnā nor Premā. Premā is married to Dānnāth, but here, unlike the earlier tale, she accepts her marriage to him with good grace and endeavors to make a success of it. A fresh element is introduced in the person of Premā's brother Kamlā Prasād, who was a nondescript figure in *Premā* but is now a scheming villain who tries to seduce Purnā when she is living with his family following her husband's death. He succeeds in enticing her into his net, but when finally he seeks to satisfy his lust, she escapes by hurling a chair at him. She takes shelter in the Widows' Home established by Amrit Rāi, spending the rest of her life in service and prayer. Amrit Rāi does not care to marry a widow because he is married to a cause—that of bringing comfort and happiness into the dismal world of Hindu widows, those luckless beings spurned and forgotten by Hindu society.

Pratigyā is a great improvement on *Premā*. The style is more chaste and elegant, the narrative more realistic and concise, the author showing greater interest in the inner workings of his characters' minds than in their outward actions. Theatrical gestures have been eliminated. But the novel still suffers from weaknesses, the earlier version hanging like a millstone round the author's neck. The marshaling of reactionary forces against Amrit Rāi was, for instance, appropriate to 1904 - 05 but it appears rather anachronistic in 1927 - 28. Similarly, though the characters in *Pratigyā* are more subtly drawn than before, the exigencies of the plot make it difficult for Prem Chand to respect their integrity. Dānnāth's doubts regarding Premā's total loyalty to him may seem psychologically real but it is hard to accept that a man with Dānnāth's capacity for friendship would allow himself to be used against his best friend by a villain like Kamlā Prasād. The incidents involving Kamlā and Purnā too, though not impossible, lack credibility.

Certain novel features in *Pratigyā* illustrate the influence of Prem Chand's audience on his treatment of the theme. The focus is now as much on man-woman relations as on the problems of the Hindu widow, and the feminists have an effective spokesperson in Sumitrā. She is the new woman conscious of her rights who refuses to be used like a doormat by her irresponsible husband. The difference in the positions of man and woman is constantly brought out: a man can remain a bachelor if he so chooses but a woman's remaining unmarried becomes an outrage and a source of scandal. Similarly, a young widow is fair game for any stud. Society employs different standards to judge the transgressions of the two sexes: the man's sin is venial while the woman's is mortal, and she has to pay a heavy price through being detested, rejected, and reviled as a strumpet and a whore.

Aside from this exposure of the double standards applied to men and women, Prem Chand does not impress us much as a social critic, by either the power of his analysis or the boldness of the solutions he suggests. Purnā's misery is alleviated first by the generosity of Lālā Badrī Prasād (an Indian version of Dickens' Mr. Brownlow and the Cheeryble brothers) and later by the Widows' Home of Amrit Rāi where she finds a permanent haven. Both these are non-solutions, because they neither take into account average human nature nor treat men and women as equals, a point on which Prem Chand is so insistent. *Premā* was, in fact, a more satisfactory work from the social point of view than is *Pratigyā*. In the former Prem Chand had shown greater courage in offering solutions to the widow problem, even going to the extent of advocating intercaste marriage; in the latter he loses himself in a mist of moral idealism.

The explanation for his change of stance is found in his letter to Rājā Raghubīr Singh of Sītāmau to which, curiously, Goyankā does not at all refer in his discussion of the novel though he himself revealed its existence.[6] His arguments in defense of Prem Chand—that he does not forbid widow marriage—look like special pleading and fail to convince. An artist's enactments should, after all, be more significant than his assertions; but here even the assertions endorse the enactment. *Pratigyā* thus, while being superior to *Premā,* is otherwise a weak novel, distinctly inferior to *Nirmalā* and the other novels of the previous decade.

III Embezzlement: *Victims of the Grand Design*

Prem Chand's bold and fearless criticism of social abuses in his novels and stories had begun to hurt, and in 1928 it involved him in a court action.[7] This action was really the culmination of a simmering anger against him in the hearts of the reactionary elements in the Hindu community, specially the Brahmins, as is evident from the impressive list of witnesses cited by the opposite party. He was accused of being anti-Brahmin, an accusation hardly justified if it implies the existence of any particular bias against any one community. Prem Chand had indeed ridiculed the sanctimonious hypocrisy and self-serving elitism of the Brahmins; but he was a social critic and had not been indulgent to other sections of society, Hindu or Muslim. He had denounced the fanaticism and bigotry of the *mullāhs* (Muslim preachers) and *maulavīs* (Muslim scholars) as well, and he had taken a peculiar delight in satirizing the weaknesses and foibles of his caste-fellows, the Kāyasthas. Bābu Bhāl Chandra, the fat, ugly, corrupt, and miserly excise official who declines to solemnize his son's marriage to Nirmalā after her father's death, is a Kāyastha. Besides exposing them in many of his short stories, he attacks them again in *Ghaban* (Embezzlement), setting off their snobbishness, their morbid concern with respectability, and their hankering for government service which made them representative of the new "educated" class, the chief victims of the Grand Design.

Ramānāth is the son of Lālā Dayānāth, a clerk in government service who gets a modest salary of fifty rupees per month. Dayānāth, unlike most other members of his class and community, is a man of scrupulous honesty who does not take bribes. As a result, he is poor. But on the occasion of his son's wedding to a beautiful girl Jālpā, the daughter of a well-to-do village functionary, he goes beyond his means and runs into debt. The only way to silence the creditors who are getting more and more restive each day is to persuade Jālpā to part with some of her ornaments, a task which Dayānāth asks his son to perform. Ramānāth has, however, portrayed before his wife an impressive picture of the family's finances—of houses, estates, bank balances—and it would now be hard to explain to her why a rich family like his must sell ornaments to meet its obligations. He is nevertheless prepared to steal them if his father approved of his doing so. The father rejects this suggestion, but when Ramā goes ahead with his plan he accepts the stolen ornaments. Jalpā, given the impression that the ornaments were stolen by a thief, is plunged into gloom and depression.

Ramā is able to find a job as a clerk in the octroi office on twenty rupees a month. But he believes in the good life himself and must also find money to satisfy the whims of his beautiful wife. So he starts taking bribes and, confident of being able to pay back from his extra income, gets ornaments for her including a *chandrahār* ("necklace") on credit. Jalpā makes friends with Ratan, the youthful wife of an old and wealthy lawyer Pandit Indu Bhushan. There has to be a rise in the standard of living to keep up with the Joneses, and all Ramā's extra income is eaten up by the couple's new style of living. Ratan likes Jalpā's bracelets and gives Ramā six hundred rupees to get the same kind made for her. Ramā asks the jeweler to make another pair, giving him the money, but the latter adjusts the money against his previous account. Months pass but there are no bracelets. Ratan is furious. Ramā, to show Ratan that he still has her money, brings the day's proceeds from the office and Jalpā, not being privy to the secret, gives the money to Ratan. Ramā has to deposit the government money by next morning or face imprisonment. He tries to raise it from his friends but, on failing to do so, runs away from home.

Ramā, traveling without a ticket, is about to be thrown out of the train when Devīdīn, an old man of about sixty, comes to his rescue, and not only lends him money but also invites him to stay with him in Calcutta. He has been making a living as a greengrocer there for the last forty years and, though a low-caste untouchable, is a man of character and convictions. His two young sons were beaten to death by the police while picketing stores selling foreign cloth. His crusty but kind old wife Jaggo looks after the shop. She is at first chilly to Ramā but later warms up and starts treating him like her own son.

Ramā, haunted by the fear of the police, rarely stirs out. He does not know that Jālpā had restored the government money by selling her ornaments and that there are no longer any charges against him.

A famous play is going to be staged in the theater, and Ramā has a keen desire to see it. He sets out to book his seat in advance but walks the street like a scared animal. Seeing three policemen heading in his direction, he tries to dodge them; the policemen, however, grow suspicious and drag him to the police station. Devīdīn appears on the scene and tries to secure his release by offering a small bribe. The police inspector demands fifty guineas. By the time Devīdīn returns with the money, the police have decided to use Ramā as a witness in a dacoity case which was fizzling out for lack of a credible witness. Ramā agrees to play the police game when he is promised handsome compensation in the form of a lucrative job after the disposal of the case. He is deterred by neither the immorality of giving false evidence nor the criminality of sending innocent people to the gallows.

Jālpā, meanwhile, through clever use of the device of a chess puzzle, succeeds in tracing Ramā. She comes to Calcutta and locates Devīdīn who tells her of Ramā's having become a police witness. She tries to make him see the light, but, owing partly to greed and partly to fear of harassment, he is unable to escape from the clutches of the police. On Ramā's testimony, five persons are sentenced to ten years' imprisonment, eight to five years; and one, Ramesh, is sentenced to death. As a restitution for Ramā's criminal conduct, Jālpā searches out Ramesh's family, collects money for it and serves it. Ramā is deeply moved when one day he sees Jālpā in a tattered *sāri* carrying a pitcher of water on her head. He decides to tell the judge the whole truth. The case against the dacoits is dismissed. Ramā and Jālpā are reconciled and, along with the widow Ratan, Devīdīn, Jaggo, and Johrā, the courtesan who was appointed to entertain Ramā during his degradation, go and settle down on the bank of the Ganges forming a utopian community away from the corruptions of city life.

Prem Chand had started work on *Ghaban* while *Pratigyā* was still being serialized in *Chānd*. According to Madan Gopāl, it was begun sometime in 1926 - 27 and finished by the end of 1928.[8] But Amrit Rāi asserts that it was written in 1929 because the dacoity case in the novel in which the police try to involve the hero Ramānāth refers to the Meerut Conspiracy Case, arrests for which were begun in March 1929. He sees a manifest difference between the first and second halves of the novel, the first half being primarily social, the second, primarily political, the middle point being reached when Ramānāth leaves Allahabad for Calcutta and Devīdīn appears.[9] The theory is not tenable, for Devīdīn's introduction seems to be integral to the original plan of the novel. Moreover, there are political elements even in the first half—Ratan's aged husband, who has spent a year in Europe, is an admirer of everything Western, an admiration which stops him neither from marrying a young girl less than half his age nor from the criminal negligence of not making a will to ensure her property rights, though he is a lawyer. This infatuation of the higher gentry with things European is contrasted with the true patriotism of a poor, low-caste man like Devīdīn who sacrifices two sons in organizing the boycott of foreign goods. Devīdīn thus appears to be integral to the thematic structure of the novel. So far as the police practice of initiating false cases against political workers is concerned, it was, as Prem Chand knew very well, quite common much before the Meerut case. In *Rangabhumi* Vinaya Singh is accused by the authorities in Udaipur of being in league with dacoits; and in *Kāyākalp* Chakradhar is charged with inciting the laborers though in actual fact he had restrained them. Also, whereas the number of those arrested in connection with the Meerut Conspiracy Case was thirty-one, there are only fourteen accused in the dacoity case in *Ghaban*. This may be a minor discrepancy but there is a major one too. Muslims constituted a sizable proportion of those accused in the Meerut case;[10] in the dacoity case in the novel Prem Chand makes no mention of the religious affiliations of the accused. It is unlikely that he would have failed to give due recognition to the Muslims for their role if he were really writing about the Meerut case. Besides, there is no mention at all of the social and political views of the accused which might denote their sympathy for communism.

Critics have interpreted the main theme of the novel in different ways, most of them emphasizing the social aspect, like the Indian women's fondness for ornaments and its disastrous consequences. Goyankā[11] has stressed the cultural aspect, placing Ramā in the line of characters like Gyān Shankar who have come under the influence of the materialistic civilization of the West,[12] predominantly an urban civilization which encourages increase in our wants and emphasizes ostentation and self-display. The universities established by the British are the prime agents in the propagation of these values among the urban middle class in India. They are little more than factories for the manufacture of graduates, and the only education they have given our young men is in self-indulgence and the aping of Western ways. Ramā, according to Goyankā, is a product of this sort of education.

Certain points, however, need clearer definition. As Goyankā knows, Ramānāth was in the college only for two months. It would therefore be hardly fair to put him in the same category as Gyān Shankar who, apart from being a graduate, is also an intellectual. University education, moreover, cannot be wholly bad. Pratāp Chandra, Vinaya Singh, Prem Shankar, and Chakradhar are all university educated people, but they are enlightened and sensible. Ramānāth, in his shiftlessness and love of ease, has greater resemblance to Virjan's husband Kamlā in *Vardān*. Like him he lacks a basic strength of character which makes him delight in low company and attach more importance to his own notion of social predominance in which ostentatious living is synonymous with high social status. The influence of Western ways is undoubtedly there but Kamlā and Ramā mainly represent the low social culture of the cities in an age of transition between the old and the new. Kamlā's diversions were those of a decadent Indian culture—kite-flying, pigeon-fancying, cock-fights, etc.; Ramā is more modern though he still enjoys chess. On the occasion of his wedding he and his friends take great interest in arranging the pomp and show which are an inseparable part of an Indian wedding and which have his father's full approval. Prem Chand's criticism is thus directed not at Western civilization alone; the Indian tradition with its vicious social customs and its effete social culture is also at fault, an indictment which is even more transparent in the account of Jālpā's upbringing. Devīdīn's story also corroborates this point; he too was led to embezzlement by his wife's fondness for ornaments.

Goyankā's comment, however—that Prem Chand evaluates the character and values of the modern youth by placing these in the context of the country's struggle for freedom—is very pertinent.[13] And, as usual, his stern moralism admits of no compromise. In *Kāyākalp* Chakradhar and Ahilyā stray from the path of duty as soon as they succumb to the temptation of worldly comfort. In *Ghaban* the degradation of Ramā goes even deeper: he becomes a traitor and an inhuman monster. The moral theme is presented even more dramatically in the conversion of Jālpā. Her "new life" begins with the symbolic act of dumping all her ornaments and fine clothes in the Ganges: "Till the middle of the night she was putting these objects aside as if she were preparing for some journey. Yes, it was really a journey—a journey from darkness to light, from falsehood to truth" (152). Ratan too has the same sense of guilt on the death of Pandit Indu Bhushan—that in her preoccupation with her own pleasure she had failed in her duty to her husband who was so deeply attached to her (195 - 96). The message is quite plain: so long as the individual is absorbed in his own pleasure-seeking and comfort, he cannot have the moral strength to serve another individual or cause.

At the social level, Prem Chand's chief target is the middle-class spirit—mammonish, mean, shallow, and servile, with its obsessive concern with respectability and its snobbishness—which had led the middle-class Indians to regard government service as the be-all and end-all of their lives. So mortally afraid are they of being confused with the working class that their entire life becomes an unremitting struggle to demonstrate their superior status and to ape the ways of the more affluent classes. They have no higher interests or aims in life and are incapable of any lofty gesture. Ramesh Bābu claims to be a friend of Ramā and plays chess with him for hours, but when Ramā is in difficulty, his straitlaced moral code does not permit him to come to his aid. Aristocrats like Rājā Bharat Singh and Rāi Kamlānand have some redeeming virtues, but the middle classes seem to have hardly any. Their mortal fear of being confused with the working classes makes it impossible for them to pursue any art or craft; the only avenue left open to them is therefore government service. The British, shrewd judges of the Indian character as they were, exploited this weakness of the middle class and bought them up by dangling before them the carrot of government service. Devīdīn's comment to Jālpā that people in her community doted on government service is both just and true (271).

There is, however, another important theme in the novel which has been practically ignored by most critics—the miserable failure of Indian males to understand women. Most Indian men, according to Prem Chand, have a poor opinion of their mates, believing that they are slaves of pleasure, mentally underdeveloped children who can be satisfied with glittering toys like gold ornaments. In *Ghaban* Prem Chand presents a rare picture of married love. The only benediction Jālpā would have asked of a deity is that she might continue to enjoy the love of her husband (125). Like other members of her sex she longed for ornaments, but she would have never accepted them if it had meant putting her husband in jeopardy. Her most serious grouse against Ramā is that he should have rated her so poorly, considered her "so mean, so selfish, so greedy" (253). This was an injustice, grave but not uncommon. Pandit Indu Bhushan too thought on the same lines, believing that a profusion of creature comforts for his wife could make up for his deficiencies in other respects. There is thus a kind of patronage but neither friendship nor companionship in an Indian middle-class marriage. By providing a contrast in the more robust relationship between Devīdīn and his wife Jaggo, Prem Chand suggests that the Doll's House image of woman is a middle-class creation, reflecting their decadence and retreat from reality. True, the women sometimes do not measure up to what they ought to be. Ratan is ignorant of realities and lives in her own dream world: she is partly responsible for her husband's failure to make a will, for the very thought of death was unpleasant to her. Even after his death, she shows little concern with her own interests. But what else could one expect from a woman with her background? This does not, however, mean that Indian women are in any way inferior either to men or to their counterparts in other lands. If anything, they are superior, for they have untapped reserves of strength which manifest themselves at moments of crises. The women in *Ghaban*—Jālpā, Ratan, Jaggo, even Johrā—are courageous and noble. Jālpā, through her determination, resourcefulness, nobility, and self-sacrifice, acts as the conscience of Ramā and brings him back to the path of duty and virtue. She is the effective protagonist, both the hero and heroine, of *Ghaban*.

From the political point of view, *Ghaban* reflects, with increasing sharpness, Prem Chand's growing disquiet at the complexion of the freedom movement which was to find eloquent expression two years later in his letter to Nigam exposing the "*bourgeois* mentality."[14] The police officers, Pandit Indu Bhushan, Ramesh Bābu, and Ramā—all are members of the educated class, convinced of their own superiority to the masses. They are, however, all sunk in the mire of their own selfishness. The questions asked by Devīdīn of the Sāhib Bahādur who was making a great ballyhoo as to what picture of *Swarāj* the latter had in mind, are profoundly disturbing and prophetic (171 - 72).

Prem Chand shows remarkable psychological insight in depicting Ramā's waverings of mind, and admirable artistic control in not portraying him as a villain. His love for Jālpā is the great redeeming trait in his otherwise weak personality. Though a well-delineated individual, Ramā is, in his weaknesses, also typical of the middle class, a product of his environment, and the victim of a malady widely prevalent. As usual, Prem Chand's ironies, predicated on a Dickensian contrast between the "respectable" rich and the "despised" poor, are amusing and disquieting. Ramā belongs to a high caste; so does the deputy-inspector of police whose respectable origin is evident from his long, shapely nose and his high forehead. But whereas they have no hesitation in taking recourse to falsehood and sending innocent men to the gallows for their own self-interest, the untouchable Devīdīn and his wife are honest, devoted, unselfish, and patriotic. The exchange between Gopī and Jālpā is instructive. Gopī asserts that "howsoever generous a *chamār* ["handler of dead cattle"] might be, he is still a *chamār.*" Jālpā's, and Prem Chand's, reply is: "I consider that *chamār* better than that Pandit who always lives off others" (238). Mani Bhushan, the nephew of Pandit Indu Bhushan, robs his uncle's helpless widow of all her property; Devīdīn and Jaggo, total strangers and low caste to boot, treat Ramānāth and Jālpā as son and daughter, standing by them through thick and thin. The latter's life with the old couple, suffused in the tender warmth of parental affection, is one of the finest things in the novel. Prem Chand's deep humanism made him derive genuine pleasure from portraying scenes like these in which human beings, transcending the barriers of caste, creed, and station, and discovering their common humanity, experience a spiritual renewal through love and friendship. *Ghaban* is an interesting and gripping story, but it is this warmth of human feeling which lifts it into the realm of art and makes it a fine novel.

CHAPTER 7

Novels of the Fourth Phase, 1929 - 36

I The Arena: *In the Footsteps of the Mahātmā*

IN *Karmabhumi* (The Arena) Prem Chand revives the pattern of his more ambitious political novels—*Premāshram* and *Rangabhumi*. In the "inner circle" it is an account of the "education" and growth of Amarkānt, another one of Prem Chand's idealistic young heroes, examined in terms of his changing relationship to the members of his family—his wife Sukhdā, his father Lālā Samarkānt, and his sister Nainā. Amarkānt's ideals and affections, which lead him to a career of public service, also involve him with other individuals—his friend and classmate Salīm, the humble Muslim girl Sakīnā, the brave Rājput woman Munnī, and the *harijans* of the village where he chooses to work. All these events are viewed in the perspective of the Indian freedom movement which had entered a more active phase about the time Prem Chand was working on this novel.

Amarkānt's moral evolution is traced in three stages. The first covers the period of his stay with his father. The second shows him breaking away first from his father, then from his wife, leaving his native city to work in the village near Hardwār. The third phase begins with his imprisonment and concludes with his release and membership in the committee chosen to negotiate with the governor. Private and public issues enmesh each other, and the mature Amarkānt, a seasoned social worker, is a much chastened figure who has got rid of his angularities and is able to establish healthy relationships with his family and friends.

The uncomfortable nature of these relationships generates the initial movement in the story. Amarkānt is a rather mediocre youth who, in spite of being twenty, has not yet got his matriculation. His father Lālā Samarkānt is a wealthy moneylender who has amassed a fortune through lending at exorbitant rates of interest and dealing in stolen goods. He is an enormous man, physically, possessing all the arrogance and bluster of a self-made man. He regards education as a waste of time and money and wants his son to assist him in the family business. The compulsion to do so becomes greater for Amar after his marriage to Sukhdā, the proud and self-willed daughter of a wealthy widow. She too puts pressure on him to stop dabbling in politics and assist his father. Amar yields to this pressure, specially when he is told that he is about to become a father. But the dubious nature of his father's business repels him and, on matriculation, he starts doing part-time work as a clerk. The Lālā is happy at the birth of a grandson, but his domineering attitude toward Amar annoys even Sukhdā, and the couple set up another household. Amar makes a living by selling *khādi* ("homespun cloth"); he carries the bundles on his back, which offends Sukhdā's sense of respectability.

Lālā Samarkānt is closefisted and unscrupulous, but he has some old-world virtues. Ever since the death of a faithful servant, a Muslim Pathān, he has supported his widow and daughter. Conveying the old widow home one evening, Amarkānt is struck by the comeliness of her daughter Sakinā. His feelings assume a dangerous intensity because he has always been treated casually by his imperious wife and is starved of love. Amar's interest in Sakinā becomes a scandal and obliges him to leave Benaras. He goes to a *harijan* village near Hardwār and devotes himself to social service.

However, before his departure from Benaras, another matter claims Amar's attention. During an educational tour of villages led by their college professor Dr. Shānti Kumār, the party was shocked to find a Rājput woman (Munnī) who had been raped by three British soldiers. A few months after this incident, the same woman stabs two Englishmen in front of Amar's father's shop. Amar takes a leading role in organizing her defense. Since her acquittal, she has been living in the *harijan* village. Munnī is a handsome Rājput woman, and Amar is atttracted to her. She reciprocates his attentions, but when the moment of decision comes Amar turns back.

Meanwhile things in the village are not going well. Hit by the Great Depression of 1929, which causes a crash in prices of their produce, the peasants are unable to pay their rents. With Amar and Swāmī Ātmānand as leaders, a movement is begun to seek reduction in rents. The Swāmī advocates an aggressive movement but Amar favors an appeal to the landlord, a wealthy and powerful abbot. Amar is also influenced in his conciliatory approach by his friend and classmate Salīm, who is now a civil service official in this district.

By this time Sukhdā too has become an active social worker. Her first plunge into public life was inspired by anger at the tyranny of high-caste Hindus in denying *harijans* entry to their temples. The agitation was a success and Sukhdā became famous. Since then she and Dr. Shānti Kumār have been agitating to get public housing for the poor. The agitation takes a serious turn and leads to many arrests, including Sukhdā's. Amar gets the news of her imprisonment and is surprised at her bravery, for he had always thought of her as a worldly creature, too selfish to be concerned with others' misery. In his exhilaration, he delivers an inflammatory speech calling upon the people to revolt. He is taken into custody by Salīm and sent to jail.

With all his near and dear ones behind bars and his daughter Nainā given away in marriage, Lālā Samarkānt undergoes a spiritual conversion. He had been mainly responsible for the excesses during the temple-entry agitation in which many low-caste people were killed by the police. His own daughter-in-law and daughter had defied him. He now softens toward Amar on Sukhdā's advice and sets out to see him in prison. First he visits the *harijan* village and brings about a reconciliation between the villagers and Salīm. He is not allowed to see Amar by the jail authorities in Lucknow.

Amar too experiences a spiritual conversion. One of his fellow prisoners is Kālé Khān, the thug who had at one time come to him to sell stolen goods. But Kālé Khān is now a changed man, intensely religious, utterly nonviolent, and ever ready to serve others. He does not so much as raise his hand when he is almost beaten to death by the jailors. Amar, impressed by his faith in God, becomes deeply religious himself.

It is now Salīm's turn to be liberated. Disgusted by the government's callous attitude to the people, he resigns his position in the civil service and becomes a servant of the villagers. A reign of terror now prevails in the countryside and the military is everywhere. Salīm too is arrested and joins Amar in the Lucknow jail. Since Munnī, Sakīnā and her mother as well as Sukhdā and her mother are all in jail, Nainā is the only one of the heroic band who has not proved herself. She surpasses everyone, however, for she is shot by her reactionary husband while leading a public demonstration. Her martyrdom brings the movement for public housing to a successful conclusion. The stalwarts of the two movements are all united in jail, and there are touching scenes of reconciliation between Amar and his father, and his wife. Even an old sinner like Lālā Dhanī Rām is converted and acts as a messenger of peace from the governor. Amar sees the hidden hand of the Almighty in these miraculous metamorphoses and turns into an apostle of peace and conciliation. Sakīnā is to be married to Salīm, and a committee of five is established to negotiate with the governor on the problems of the villagers.

Karmabhumi was written between 1929 and 1931, being published in 1932.[1] It is a difficult novel to assess. The most striking commentary is Rāmvilās Sharmā's, though it raises more questions than it answers. He sees Prem Chand's portrayal of Amarkānt ironic to the point of sarcasm, an interpretation which would make him more of an antihero than a hero. Sharmā has no doubt that Amar is being used by the author to expose the spuriousness and hollowness of the bourgeoisie's professed concern for the have-nots. For him the novel ends with the martyrdom of the villagers, victims of inhuman repression at the hands of the foreign rulers. The rest, depicting Amar's spiritual regeneration and his acceptance of the philosophy of forgiveness and conciliation, is irrelevant.[2]

This interpretation is hard to accept, whatever our critical approach—whether we take into account the intentions of the author or treat the work as an artistic whole respecting its integrity and autonomy. *Karmabhumi* is mainly an "education" novel, a *Bildungsroman*, the story of a young man's coming into his own despite adverse forces of heredity and environment. About two-thirds of the text is, as Goyankā points out, devoted to the story of Amarkānt.[3] Amar is rather unique among Prem Chand's heroes in that he does not emerge as a finished product from the hands of his creator. It is therefore ironic that Prem Chand's scientific portrayal of his hero's moral evolution should invite the suspicion of lack of sympathy toward him. Amar is an erring, imperfect human being, but there is little doubt of his essential decency and honesty of purpose. He has ideals and principles but lacks the moral strength to stick to them in an unflinching manner. The causes of his weakness lie in his upbringing and early environment. Being starved of affection—he has lost his mother while still a child—he is susceptible to the slightest exhibition of kindliness and love. He is stubborn to the people who are hard to him but extremely pliant to those who treat him kindly. Thus he resists his father, who tries to bully him into the family business, and Sukhdā, who wants him to become a man of the world, but he allows himself to be manipulated by his mother-in-law Renukā, the Mahant (Abbot), by Gazanavī and, finally, by Seth Dhanī Rām. The same weakness explains his involvement with Sakīnā and with Munnī, and the extraordinary onrush of religiosity on witnessing Kālé Khān's dramatic transmutation. Prem Chand exposes the weaknesses in his character, but there should be no doubt of his sympathetic attitude toward his hero and approval of the direction in which he is moving. Renukā's influence is, for instance, not entirely harmful. She contributes to his cultivation and emotional development: the awkward, tense, and nervous youth now becomes more relaxed. Prem Chand is as critical of his rigidity and inflexibility as of his irresolution and vacillation. The latter is in a way a consequence of the former, of the impossibly rigid standards he sets for himself. He refuses to work with Dr. Shānti Kumār in the school because the doctor hesitates to resign his professorship which brings in a good income and makes it possible for him to finance the school. "He had not yet learned," Prem Chand says of Amar, "to compromise with principles. It was because he had never been placed in situations which bring flexibility in our nature after we have entered the world of action and have had the bitter experience of life" (108). Shānti Kumār speaks for the author when he tells Amar: "Our lives are based on compromise. You may think of me as you please but the time will come when your eyes will be opened and you will realize that the importance of reality in life is not an iota less than that of the ideal" (109). Different though it may sound from Chakradhar's condemnation of the brutality of fact in *Kāyākalp*, it is Prem Chand's voice nonetheless. That Shānti Kumār is acting as his spokesman is proved by Salīm's ridiculing of the school and Sukhdā's open hostility. Sakīnā, on the other hand, takes the doctor's side, whose words are prophetic: the time does come when Amar's eyes are opened, when he recognizes the importance of the real and learns the wisdom of compromise.

Sukhdā's moral evolution supports the above interpretation. As soon as she hears of Lālā Samarkānt's illness, she goes to look after him and stays with him until he is well, but Amar does not go. Prem Chand's criticism of the latter's rigidity is apparent in his praise of Sukhdā: "there was tenderness in her pride . . ." (128), a quality lacking in Amar's. Amar is not devoid of virtues, however. As Sukhdā becomes more mature and chastened, she moves closer to him and develops a better appreciation of his merits. She understands the cause of his leaving home, which was more like a boardinghouse to him (216). By the time she leaves for prison, she is "a follower of her husband" (276). It is at her suggestion that Lālā

Samarkānt goes to see Amar when the latter is in jail, thus preparing the ground for the eventual reconciliation between father and son.

Like Prem Chand's other novels, *Karmabhumi* faithfully reflects the current political situation in the country. Indian politics had moved fast during the years 1929 to 1931. The Lahore Congress had, under the presidentship of Jawāharlāl Nehru, declared the achievement of complete independence for India as its goal on 31 December 1929. On 11 March 1930 Gandhi had started the Salt Satyāgraha, which led to his own arrest and that of about 60,000 other people. Meanwhile, as a result of the Round Table Conference held in London, the British Government had conceded full provincial autonomy and the gradual introduction of responsible government at the center. The Indian Government had, in order to improve the political atmosphere, released Gandhi and the other Congress leaders in January 1931. The Gandhi-Irwin negotiations, begun on 17 February 1931, had concluded with the Pact on 4 March.

The Pact had a mixed reception. Jawāharlāl Nehru was sharply critical but there were many who supported it. Prem Chand was among the latter. He had, during these years, almost blind faith in Gandhi, and the adverse criticism to which the Mahātmā was subjected made it all the more urgent for Prem Chand to rally round him. *Karmabhumi* is thus permeated with the spirit of Gandhism as Prem Chand understood it. His support of Gandhi is confirmed by his discursive writings in which a marked change of tone is noticeable beginning in February 1931. Prem Chand is almost in a state of euphoria: a new era had dawned not only in the political history of India but of the world; the Hindu-Muslim question has been solved because the Muslim youth (Salīm and Sakīnā) have amply demonstrated their patriotism. So also have women (Sukhdā, Nainā, Munnī, Salonī, Sakīnā, Renukā, and Sakīnā's mother, the Pathānī). In fact, their record is even more glorious than that of the men.[4]

In the face of this overwhelming evidence, interpretations like those of Rāmvilās Sharmā seem to be far off the mark and betray a grave misunderstanding of the novel. It is, however, this very euphoria and this doctrinal enthusiasm which impair *Karmabhumi* by turning it into a tract. The plot of the story is too dominant: there is a neatness about it which is unnatural and contrived. The characters are predictable and move in directions which can be anticipated and forecast. Prem Chand shows psychological insight in their portrayal, particularly in that of Amarkānt, but the sudden conversions they undergo appear improbable and unconvincing. He fails to discriminate between the good and the bad, so much so that even old sinners and toadies like Seth Dhanī Rām turn out to be saints. The Seth's central role in bringing about the compromise with the governor would suggest that the policy of toadyism was really a wise one because it kept open the channels of communication between the freedom-fighters and the foreign rulers and made mutual understanding possible. Prem Chand is so much under the spell of his own version of Gandhism that he sees a potential saint in every self-seeker and unprincipled opportunist. His approach raises serious doubts whether he had a consistent and coherent social philosophy, that is, whether it was anything more than a vague moral idealism based on an evangelical faith in personal conversion. What a happy place the world would be if human beings could only cast out pride and envy and imbibe goodwill, generosity, humility, kindliness, and love; if the rich had more sympathy and consideration for the poor, and the poor were more deferential and humble toward the rich! This is Prem Chand's message in the novel, betraying the yawning gap between the vehemence of the rhetoric and the staidness of the solutions he offers. Amarkānt's demonstrative religiosity and faith in the benevolence of the Creator have a false ring. Also, they do not amount to much if the "converted" Amarkānt is to do little more than emphasize the sacredness of the law of contract and glorify the spirit of compromise. What a far cry it all is from the dignified rebelliousness of Surdās, his refusal to take cognizance of the unjust man-made law because it contravened the law of *dharma*!

II The Giving of the Cow: *The Meaning of Life*

Godān (The Giving of the Cow) is the story of a peasant couple's struggle for survival. Horī Rām is a small farmer in Belārī village in Uttar Pradesh who owns about an acre of land on which he is hardly able to support his family—his wife Dhaniā, his son Gobardhan and his daughters Sonā and Rupā. The land is fertile and the family is hard-working, but so enmeshed are they in the coils of debt that they have been reduced virtually to the status of bonded labor.

Horī is a typical Indian farmer; so are his dreams and aspirations. His most cherished wish is to own a cow, so that he might be able to provide milk for his family and be regarded as a respectable householder and an estimable member of his community. An opportunity to do so comes his way through the matrimonial yearnings of Bholā, a widowed milkman of advanced middle age. Hoping that Horī will be able to find a wife for him, Bholā offers him a beautiful cow of excellent breed. Horī hesitates to accept because he has no money to pay for the cow but, at Bholā's insistence, agrees to take it. The cow arrives, and the family is full of excitement. The whole village comes to congratulate Horī except his two younger brothers, Hīrā and Shobhā, whom he and his wife Dhaniā had raised. They are married now and maintain separate households. So intense is the jealousy of Hīrā that one night he poisons the cow. Horī sees Hīrā in his compound, but the latter explains his presence by saying that he had come to collect some fire from Horī's oven. However, when the cow is dead, Horī's suspicion naturally falls on Hīrā. He shares the secret with Dhaniā after extracting the promise that she would not let it out. Dhaniā makes the promise but breaks it immediately, outraged as she is by Hīrā's crime and the ingratitude and jealousy it displayed. Horī is so incensed that he beats her. There is a terrible scene in front of the entire village. Hīrā vanishes. The police inspector makes his appearance as soon as he hears of the incident. Bent on extracting money, he threatens to conduct a search of Hīrā's house. Horī is deeply perturbed—after all Hīrā is his brother and a search of his house would be a slur on the family's good name. He denies having seen Hīrā in his compound but the inspector does not budge from his decision. The village worthies advise Hori to offer a bribe but he has no money. They advance a loan out of which the inspector is to be paid, the worthies too taking their share. Dhaniā, however, upsets all their plans and exposes these sharks. The inspector retires, disgraced and angry.

Horī had despatched his son Gobar to fetch the cow from Bholā's house. There the boy saw Bholā's daughter Jhuniā, a sexy young widow, and succumbed to her charms. Jhuniā becomes pregnant and seeks shelter with Horī and Dhaniā after Gobar has absconded. They upbraid her at first but, taking pity on her, give her shelter. This is regarded as an offense against the community, and the village worthies impose on Horī a heavy fine of eighty rupees, which they pocket themselves.

Bholā has not yet been paid for his cow. He is burning with the desire of revenge against Horī because the latter's son Gobar has disgraced his family by his affair with Jhuniā. He insults Horī and demands his money, threatening to take away his pair of bullocks as compensation. Horī cannot believe that Bholā would be so mean and tells him to take the team away if his *dharma* allowed him to do so. Bholā, refusing to be deterred by any such considerations, walks away with the bullocks. Horī is now in dire straits: he cannot plough his land and has to work as a common laborer on others' farms. His family is starving. Hīra's wife Puniyā, however, comes to the family's help and gives them grain. Pandit Dātā Dīn uses Horī's weak position to strike a bargain with him: he would help Horī cultivate his own land in return for half the share of the produce.

Horī is head over ears in debt. The thirty rupees borrowed from Dulārī Sahuāin five years ago have now increased to 150; the fifty rupees taken from Mangru Sāh about ten years ago to 300; and the thirty rupees from Pandit Dātā Dīn, taken about eight years ago, are now 200. He owes money to Jhingurī Singh and Nokhé Rām too. Horī has paid them from time to time but at 30 to 60 percent compound interest the amount keeps on multiplying. He has pinned great hopes on the sugarcane crop, which is unusually good, but when the time for selling comes, out of 150 rupees that Horī gets, Jhingurī Singh takes away 125. Horī puts the balance of twenty-five rupees in Nokhé Rām's hand and returns home empty-handed! When Dhaniā comes to know of these transactions, she is mad with rage.

Gobar, after leaving Jhuniā in front of his parents' house, had gone to the big city to make money. He has been living in Lucknow for about a year and has done rather well. Starting as a day laborer he has become a small tradesman and has also saved some money. He visits his village, bringing presents for everyone in the family. Having imbibed new ideas, he is determined to insult the village sharks. Using his conversational skills, he brings back Horī's pair of bullocks from Bholā and, lionized by the village youth, organizes a fete on the occasion of the Holī festival. There is much drinking of *bhāng* (Indian hemp), singing, dancing, and amateur theatricals in which the village worthies are ridiculed. The latter are furious and plan revenge. Gobar offers to pay back his father's debt provided the lenders charged legitimate interest. In his conceit he rebukes his father for his meek submissiveness and says some harsh things to his mother. He departs, taking his wife Jhuniā and son Mangal with him and leaving a trail of bitterness behind.

The village worthies act as censors of public morals but their own morals are far from impeccable. Pandit Dātā Dīn is a venerable but wily old Brahmin whose son Mātā Dīn has seduced an innocent *chamār* girl, Siliā. She lives in a shack outside the Pandit's house and works like a slave. Mātā Dīn sleeps with her but does not take the food touched by her. He bathes and performs regularly his rituals which guard his status as a Brahmin. The *chamārs* of Siliā's family are, however, smarting under the affront to their honor by Mātā Dīn. One day they come in a group and force a bone into his mouth. This is their way of making him a *chamār*. They also try to drag Siliā away but she refuses to go. The old Pandit is disgraced and he kicks Siliā out. The poor girl, pregnant and having no place to go, is offered shelter by the kindhearted Dhaniā over objections by Horī, who is afraid of annoying the Pandit.

Sonā is now seventeen and must be married. She has been engaged to the son of a well-to-do farmer. Horī approaches Dulārī Sahuāin for a loan and is deeply touched when she agrees to give one. Sonā, aware of the family's desperate financial position, sends a message to her affianced through Siliā asking him not to demand a dowry. A letter is received by Horī in which the groom's father asks Horī not to incur unnecessary expenses. Horī is delighted and immediately runs home to inform Dhaniā who, very strangely, tells the messenger that they would do things according to tradition. Dulārī Sahuāin's promise to advance money to Horī was based on the expectation that Horī would pay back the previous loan from his excellent sugarcane crop. But the cane harvest is once again taken away by another creditor, Mangru Sāh, and Horī has nothing left to himself. Dulārī refuses to give him the loan. He is deeply worried but Nohrī comes to his help. She is the second wife of Bholā and is now living as the mistress of Nokhé Rām, the *zamindār's* steward. She is a woman of easy virtue and, under normal circumstances, Horī and Dhaniā would never have accepted her offer of money. But they are in serious trouble and cannot afford to say no.

Sonā's marriage is somehow solemnized, but Hori's position continues to deteriorate. The crops have been failing and the rent has not been paid for three years. Now even the land, the last vestige of his status as an independent cultivator, is about to be taken away when Pandit Dātā Dīn comes with a proposition which would ensure the marriage of his youngest daughter Rupā as well as save his land. This could be done if he agreed to marry her to a middle-aged farmer named Rām Dīn. Horī at first recoils from the idea of selling his daughter but the more he thinks about it, the more he is inclined to accept. Rupā is married to Rām Dīn and Horī receives 200 rupees, which he uses to pay the rent. Though Horī had entered into this transaction, his conscience had been chiding him. He explains his conduct to Gobar, who advises him not to torment himself and to try to pay back the money to Rām Dīn. Gobar had left his son Mangal with Hori and the child's presence revives in him the desire for a cow. He accepts work as a day laborer digging gravel for road construction under the scorching summer sun. At night he makes ropes, taking only a few hours' rest. One day he has a sunstroke and is dying. Dhaniā is informed and rushes to his side. Hīrā, who is back now and is pardoned by Horī, advises Dhaniā to give a cow to ensure peace for Horī's soul. Dhaniā has no money. She brings the 20 annas she had earned by making ropes and places them in Horī's cold hands, saying to Pandit Dātā Dīn: "Respected Sir, there is neither cow nor calf nor coin in the house. This is all the money; this is *his* giving of the cow." With these words she collapses.

Parallel to the world of the village is the world of the city. The link between the two is provided by Rāi Sāhib, the landlord who gets money from the village but spends it in the city. Among the other luminaries are Mr. B. Mehtā, professor of philosophy in the university and a distinguished intellectual; Mr. Khannā, manager of a bank and managing director of a sugarmill; Mr. Tankhā, a political operator; and Pandit Onkār Nāth, an opportunistic editor of a news daily. Among the women are Mr. Khannā's wife, Govindī, and Mālatī, a foreign-trained doctor and liberated woman who consorts with men on equal terms.

The life of the city is full of intrigue and manipulation, Mehtā and Govindī being the outstanding exceptions to the general degradation. Rāi Sāhib is a wealthy and cultivated landlord who squeezes his tenants to maintain his elegant and ostentatious style of life. He has carefully hedged his bets, having done a two-year stint in jail in connection with the freedom movement. He is anxious to be known as a liberal but is really a chip off the old block. When he learns of the village worthies' realization of the fine of eighty rupees from Horī, he insists on having the money himself instead of reprimanding them for this felonious exaction. But when Onkār Nāth the newsman comes to know of this action and threatens to expose him, he panics and silences the newsman by offering him a bribe. Khannā is a typical product of the commercial civilization, his sole end in life being to make money. The influence of his distorted sense of values is seen in his personal life: he ill-treats his faithful and talented wife Govindī and runs after the flamboyant and flirtatious Mālatī. Mehtā is the philosopher and intellectual who, in spite of his thorough acquaintance with Western thought and culture, is deeply committed to Indian values. It is through his influence that Mālatī is converted from a shallow, snobbish, and showy butterfly into a mature and thoughtful woman who uses her talents to serve the poor.

Godān, the last novel Prem Chand was able to complete before his death, was written between January 1932 and December 1935 or January 1936.[5] It is regarded by most critics as Prem Chand's masterpiece and one of the greatest novels ever published in Hindi. Its greatness is, however, more easily asserted than defined.

According to Rāmvilās Sharmā, the main problem of *Godān* is the problem of debt and Rāmdīn Gupt agrees with him. Goyankā, however, believes that "The aim of *Godān* is to give a realistic account of the collapse of an agricultural civilization." It is not, like *Karmabhumi,* the product of particular happenings in the age but a moving expression of some deep and solemn anguish piling up bit by bit in the author's consciousness. Horī is born out of this deep and long-standing anguish.[6]

There is a great deal of truth in Goyankā's remarks. The life and destiny of the Indian farmer are the central objects of Prem Chand's concern in *Godān*. "In a predominantly agricultural country like India, agriculture," as he says in *Karmabhumi,* "is not merely a means of livelihood; it is also an object of esteem. To be known as a householder is a matter of pride. Having lost everything as a householder, the farmer goes abroad; when he has made money, he comes back and establishes himself as a householder again. Love of honour and prestige is uppermost in his mind as it is in that of other people. He wants to live and die as a householder" (289). Obviously, the farmer's status as an independent and respectable householder depends on his possession of land. Loss of land is a fall from grace—the loss of his status as a free man and degradation into servitude and mean labor. To Prem Chand it is much more than an individual loss: it is a national disaster and tragedy, for it represents the extinction of a way of life and a system of values which are a vital part of India's cultural inheritance. *Godān* is a classic account of the shattering of the Indian farmer's dreams and aspirations and the disintegration of the social, economic, and cultural fabric of Indian civilization which this shattering represents.

In *Karmabhumi* Prem Chand had presented certain aspects of the freedom struggle in town and country, concluding the work on a note of optimism, for he saw hopeful signs of an understanding developing between the rulers and the ruled and of a growing awareness among the privileged classes of the problems of their less fortunate brethren. But we notice a distinct change of mood soon after, as reflected in his comments on current affairs. He is now inclined to question his earlier assumptions and ask some hard questions. Freedom, certainly; but freedom for whom? Was India really a nation that it could demand freedom and, having got it, preserve it? ". . . we merely shout 'nation', 'nation,' " he writes on 8 January 1934, "[but] our hearts are still plunged in the darkness of caste distinctions. . . . Who does not know that caste distinctions and nationhood are opposed to each other like poison and nectar." He was particularly riled by charges that he was anti-Brahmin and stung into stating: "If we had strength enough, we would have devoted our entire life to freeing the Hindu community from the pest of the *purohits, pujāries* (members of the Brahmin priestly class) and others who trade in religion. This two-bit gang is the most detestable leprosy, the most shameful blot on the Hindu community. Like a mammoth leach, it is sucking its blood. This is the greatest obstacle in our progress to nationhood." It was Prem Chand's firm belief that strengthening of the feeling of equality was the first condition of nationhood and that it was difficult to think of a nation in the absence of this feeling.[7] *Godān* shows us a fragmented society which has a long way to go before it can become a nation, a society divided against itself, in which there is no sense of common purposes or goals and exploitation and injustice—social, economic, and political—are a way of life.

Injustices of this kind had always aroused Prem Chand's anger and he presents a vivid picture of these in *Godān*. But he goes further and uncovers the ideology and the polity which, instead of condemning, gave them social and moral sanction. Brahminism, which lays down in *Varnāshramadharma* (four-fold division of an individual's life into stages and of society into castes, with duties corresponding to each state) the law for all sorts and conditions of men and prescribes the proper mode of social organization, is this polity. There is no respect for man as man either in the law it lays down or in the world it has brought into existence. The village worthies through their usurious practices not only drive Horī to destitution; they deprive Bholā of his dignity and honor by allowing Nokhé Rām to wrest his wife from him just as they allow Mātā Dīn to rob the *chamārs* of their honor by seducing the innocent Siliā.

The cool self-assurance and clear consciences with which the high-caste elite commit or acquiesce in these crimes shows the scant regard they have for the honor and dignity of their lower-caste fellows. Can such a society ever become a nation? Can one have any respect for the polity which turns a blind eye to injustices of this kind?

It is a decadent and corrupt world in which traditional institutions and beliefs such as religion which had taught men to cherish kindliness and compassion have lost all meaning, being reduced to little more than ritual. New modes of thought and belief like nationalism have fared no better. Patriotism has become as much a ritual as religion. The latter means *pujā* (the ritualistic aspect of worship) and *tilak* (mark on the forehead); the former jail-going and *khādi* (homespun cloth). Neither of them pays attention to the happiness and welfare of man. Prem Chand shows in his political criticism once again the sophistication and maturity of outlook which was visible in earlier masterpieces like *Rangabhumi* and *Ghaban*, but which was singularly lacking in *Karmabhumi*. Patriotism is no longer the general rubric which sanctifies every sinner; often it turns out to be the last refuge of the scoundrel, the self-seeking opportunist who cautiously hedges his bets and prepares himself for eventualities of every kind. Rāi Sāhib, Khannā, and Onkār Nāth are all patriots of this brand. Through their portrayal Prem Chand demonstrates his awareness of the extent to which the freedom movement had become infiltrated by opportunists.

In his social criticism too he has moved considerably ahead. This is reflected in his treatment of the East-West theme, projected here through the characters of Mehtā and Mālatī. Mehtā's high regard for Govindī is an indication of Prem Chand's unequivocal commitment to Indian values and culture, but he seems hesitant to assert that Western influence is entirely bad and the Indian entirely good. The Western-oriented Mālatī and Mehtā display a higher sense of responsibility than Indian aristocrats like Rāi Sāhib, Rājā Suryapratāp Singh, and Rāi Sāhib's son-in-law, Digvijaya Singh. The village notables too are all dishonest and decadent, being directly responsible through their tyranny and exploitation for the desperate economic and social plight of the Indian peasant. The *Rāj* is indeed there to give moral and legal protection to their oppressive regime, but given the type of persons they are, it is doubtful if things would have been different were they themselves the rulers of the country. *Godān* depicts the traditional fabric of Indian society cracking under the impact of the commercial civilization. In *Rangabhumi*, *Premāshram*, and *Karmabhumi*, though the villagers quarrel with one another, they also have brotherliness and fellow-feeling which come to the fore in times of misfortune. In *Godān* most of them remain selfish, mean, and unrepentant till the end. There are conversions like that of Mātā Dīn, but they are strictly of a moral and personal nature and do not lead to reorientation of social and economic relationships. Mālatī, in her attempt to reach out to the villagers, is probably the only exception, but she is a city bird, a modern woman, wholly outside the traditional Indian world of the village.

Prem Chand describes in *Godān* the harmful effect of city life—the alienation of modern man brought about by industrialism—of which he had furnished the earliest sketch in *Rangabhumi*. Gobar experiences the degrading influence of life in the slums; starts drinking and beats Jhuniā, the two of them being ever ready "to pounce on each other like hunting dogs" (266). But the degradation affects the village too. Most of the village worthies keep mistresses, Nokhé Rām's being the most blatant example. Horī's anguish at the indifference of the villagers when Nohrī beats her husband Bholā suggests Prem Chand's own at this sad decline of moral and social norms.

Money plays an important role in the novel, being used both as object and symbol. It is the common mode of restitution for offenses. Horī has given refuge to Jhuniā and he must pay money; Mātā Dīn has been polluted and he must pay money to the learned Brahmins to regain his Brahminhood. Dhaniā gives money to Dātā Dīn because it is not the cow but the money that he wanted. Onkār Nāth is silenced by the Rāi Sāhib with money. Gobar's head is turned when he has money; so also is Nohrī's. And Horī can save his plot of land only by selling his daughter Rupā for money.

Rāmdīn Gupt has complained that Prem Chand does not offer any solution for the peasant's sad plight. The peasant is angry with his lot but makes no effort to get organized and free himself from exploitation. From this point of view he finds the peasants of the earlier novels more united, organized, and hopeful about their future. He sees signs of hope from Gobar, taking him as representative of the new generation.[8] But Gobar too does not come up to the level of Balrāj in *Premāshram* or even of Munnī in *Karmabhumi*. The peasants' lack of initiative reflects Prem Chand's growing pessimism about the future and his loss of faith in the kind of utopian solutions he had offered in his previous novels. One of the reasons for the peasants' inaction may be that, whereas in the earlier novels they get leadership and direction from the middle-class idealists and intellectuals, it is not forthcoming in this novel. Mehtā is high-minded and noble but his concerns—whether cultural or social—are almost exclusively philosophical. Prem Chand's criticism of Mehtā is extremely guarded, but there is no question that he illustrates the olympian indifference, or at best the sentimental sympathy, of the intellectuals when more than three-fourths of the country's population was being driven by tyranny and oppression to the verge of extinction. Mehtā and Mālatī do evince some sympathy for the peasants but they have no coherent program of political or social action which might ensure the latter's survival.

Though Prem Chand is critical of them, their limitations are in a way his own. Musing on the peasants' sad lot, Mālatī thinks that "their narrow-mindedness and selfishness was to a large extent the cause of their miserable condition" (293). But analyzing her friend's thinking on the next page, Prem Chand says "Mehtā did not have the courage to face the truth that their angelic nature was the very cause of their plight. Alas! if only these people were more of men and less of angels, they would not have been kicked around like this" (294). The inconsistency in his thinking which these two judgments demonstrate is a reflection of the tension in Prem Chand's mind between revolutionary activism and Gandhian idealism. This is the chief reason why, in spite of his passionate identification with the common man, he is unable to suggest a concrete and clear course of social action. He is above all a moralist, but moral conversions like those of Mālatī, Khannā, Mātā Dīn, and Gobar have unfortunately never solved social and economic problems.

There are other considerations too which inhibit Prem Chand from offering revolutionary solutions. Horī and Dhaniā are weak and helpless but they embody an essential decency and nobility which they have inbibed from millenia of Indian culture. They provide sanctuary to Jhuniā and Siliā when everyone else has abandoned them. Horī forgives even Hīrā who had brought so much misery on his head. If the Indian peasant became violent and aggressive, he might succeed in gaining his legitimate rights, but he would lose the humanity and goodness which have constituted his great distinction. In a world overwhelmed by moral decay and disintegration, Horī retains his *dharma* and his sense of discrimination between right and wrong. It would be a sad day for India, Prem Chand felt, if these noble virtues were to disappear. The worth of any doctrine or tradition, he believed, must be assessed by its role in the promotion of life and happiness. He adopts an empirical and existentialist approach, distrusting all attempts to construct morality *a priori*. The ground of his humanist ethics is not what God wills or tradition dictates but what is good for man. His attitude to tradition is ambivalent. There is a living tradition which puts man in touch with the spiritual inheritance of mankind and helps him complete his moral growth. It raises him above the level of his selfish and narrow concerns and teaches him to place the good of others above his own. There is the dead tradition which shuts him into the strait jacket of outworn customs and institutions, inhibiting him and frustrating his growth and fulfillment. Horī's conception of *dharma* leads him to give equal respect to both kinds of tradition but Dhaniā's attitude is more independent and critical. This golden-hearted and brave woman shines above all others in a sea of mediocrity and brainlessness. Her sturdy common sense revolts against the idea of plunging herself in deeper misery by taking another loan to give away a cow when her husband is dying. "Was her whole duty to keep crying for the man who was her life companion?" "Life" is the key word here. Is "life" synonymous with "crying"? Does it mean nothing more? Is it possible that the man who was her life companion would wish her to deny it and resign herself to death by assuming the burden of further debt? Dhaniā's answer is emphatically in the negative.

Godān is a great novel though it has certain weaknesses. In spite of Goyankā's heroic efforts to demonstrate the unity of the two worlds of town and country, they do not fuse as they do in *Premāshram* and *Karmabhumi* but rather exist apart from each other. It is even harder to accept Goyankā's contention that town life is used by the author to show the purity, selflessness, and humanity of country life.[9] Prem Chand's faith in man is firm but he does not indulge in the facile moralism which leads some writers to glorify poverty and suffering. He is fully aware of the crushing effect of poverty and the deterioration of character it brings about. Speaking of the disheartened and demoralized peasants whom the burden of debt and the tyranny of the elite have reduced to a benumbed existence, he says: "You can make them behave dishonestly for a half-penny, take to fighting with sticks for a handful of grain. It is the limit of degradation when a man forgets all about his honour and dignity" (336).[10]

Of course, some can retain their honor even in misfortune and one of Prem Chand's striking successes in the novel is the tragic dignity which Horī attains. The great classical artists recognized that the world is not made for man but showed that man could achieve dignity in that world. Prem Chand, with his positive acceptance of life, might not accept the first assertion but he does believe that man could achieve dignity in this world through his courage, nobility, and above all his spirit of self-sacrifice, as Horī does. We are made to feel that he is superior to his oppressors: "a vanquished prince who had enclosed himself in his fort of an acre of land and was trying to guard it as his own life" (331). He is a picture of dignity and decorum who, like Wordsworth's Michael, labors to preserve the bond of natural piety by working to buy a cow for his grandson, and who, like the Leech-gatherer, refuses to allow his enfeebled body to subdue his tenacious spirit. He is not a winner in the battle of life but he does not give up the struggle till death overtakes him.

The dominant emotion of the novel is, however, not pity but anger, personified not in Horī but in Dhaniā. Prem Chand sympathizes with Horī but he admires and adores Dhaniā. Her roughness and lack of refinement are inevitable in a woman of her social background, but she has a sharp intelligence (42) which enables her to probe into the real motives of hypocritical well-wishers, a moral courage like that of a lioness (45) which, combined with her heart of gold, makes her despise public opinion in doing what she believes to be right. Her generosity to Jhuniā could be explained away to some extent as an attempt to cover up the indiscretions of her own son, but that to Siliā is an intensely human and heroic act when all the power and wealth of the village is ranged against her. In her stinging rebuke to the "leaders" of the village she acts as the spokesman of the author: "These butchers, these suckers of the poor man's blood, are the headmen of the village. Through interest, loansharking, forced presents, bribery, and corruption they fleece the poor. On top of this they want *swarāj*. But *swarāj* won't be won by going to jail; it will be won through *dharma*, through justice" (110).

It is not without significance that she is the last one to stay in our minds when the novel ends. Her courageous and sensible act in refusing to be stampeded into giving a cow contains the message of the novel. The question in her mind regarding Horī continues to haunt us. Is it really the meaning of love, of human life to be eternally in debt and to be working like slaves for others' benefit?

III Mangal-Sutra: *The Spirit of the Age*

Mangal-Sutra (The Auspicious Bond) is the story of Pandit Dev Kumār, a distinguished author and intellectual who has decided to retire from the life of active creative labor and involvement in the world. He has a wife, two sons—Sant Kumār and Sādhu Kumār—and a daughter, Pankajā. Sant Kumār's wife Pushpā is another member of the family. The two brothers provide a study in contrast. Both are intelligent and handsome but while Sant Kumār is arrogant, unscrupulous, greedy, and ambitious, Sadhu Kumār is sober, upright, humane, and idealistic, having given up his studies in connection with the freedom movement and served two prison terms.

Sant Kumār has been trained as a lawyer but could never get started in the profession. All his energies, therefore, are directed toward recovering the property which his father had sold about twenty years ago at a throw-away price but which is now worth ten times more. He consults his friend Mr. Sinhā, a brilliant lawyer. Sinhā's advice is very simple—if it could be established that Dev Kumār was not sane at the time he sold the property, the whole transaction could be declared null and void. This could be established with the help of some witnesses and a medical certificate from a doctor holding an official position, a civil surgeon. Sinhā advises Sant Kumār also to make friends with Tibbī, the sharp, witty, and attractive daughter of the subjudge who would be trying the Kumār case. He would have been glad to perform this service for his friend himself had he not been busy courting the pale-faced daughter of the civil surgeon, Mr. Kāmat, whose help was needed in the murder case Mr. Sinhā was arguing.

If the esteem and regard a man has been able to win from his children is a test of his having had a successful life, Pandit Dev Kumār's life has not been a success. Sādhu Kumār and Pankajā respect him but Sant Kumār is rude and insulting. Ridiculing the old man's idealism and lack of worldly wisdom, he sarcastically refers to him as "a saint" who had ruined his children's prospects by squandering the family fortune. As soon as Sant Kumār and his friend have finalized their plan, they go and place it before Pandit Dev Kumār who can hardly believe his ears. He refuses to have anything to do with such an unprincipled scheme. But Sinhā and Sant Kumār have implanted a seed in the Pandit's mind and it grows. Finally, he comes to the conclusion that consideration of right and wrong are irrelevant in this amoral world. He goes out and meets Seth Giridhar Dās to whom he had sold his land many years ago. The Seth doubts the Pandit's sanity and unceremoniously dismisses him.

Dev Kumār's mind is, however, made up. When Sant Kumār and Sinhā come to see him he himself asks them as to when they are going to file the suit. They are elated. But the question is where the money is to come from to meet the costs of the suit, for Dev Kumār had led a detached life and never cared very much for money. But he has a large circle of admirers who have been anxious to show their respect for him in a concrete manner. One of these suggests that a purse be presented to Pandit Dev Kumār on the occasion of his sixtieth birthday. Soon a committee is formed under the chairmanship of a Rājā to collect the money and to organize the function. Dev Kumār has some compunctions of conscience in being the subject of publicity and also in accepting money which was not a product of his hard labor. He is therefore a bit worried and downcast on the day of the function. Soon, however, a ray of light is visible on his pensive, wan countenance. This purse, he has succeeded in persuading himself, is his provident fund, the legitimate reward of his service to the community for the last forty years. And so when the Rājā presents it to him, there is pride, joy, and victory on his face.

Mangal-Sutra is the fragment of the novel Prem Chand wrote in 1936, between June and October when he was critically ill. Published for the first time in 1948, it is an extremely important work written by him as it were in his own blood. It is therefore unfortunate that critics have practically ignored it and that hardly a single worthwhile assessment of the novel is available. Though he was able to write only four chapters, there is a certain roundness about it which gives clear indications of Prem Chand's way of thinking and encourages critical evaluation.

As the title indicates, the novel is concerned with bonds —between parents and children, husband and wife, lover and beloved, master and servant, and between the author and his public. Prem Chand's object is to present a society in which all these auspicious and sacred bonds have been vitiated by the rampant spirit of commercialism. For Sant Kumār parenthood is meaningful only insofar as it can be translated in terms of money. Pandit Dev Kumār is a renowned and respected man who has brought up his family with love and affection and is still devoted to it. Any son could have been proud of such a father. But he is no longer putting money in the family chest and has therefore no value in Sant Kumār's eyes. "I feel like shooting him; I do not consider him my father but my enemy," he says.[11] His attitude to his wife is no different. Pushpā does not earn; she is therefore a dependent and ought to accept her subordinate status. Just as he interprets his relationship to his father in terms of money, he asks Pushpā to get him ten thousand rupees as a loan from her father who is a prosperous physician. Pushpā's reluctance to do so leads him to threaten her with separation. Obviously the sacred bond of marriage has no meaning for him.

All human relationships tend to be conceived in commercial terms. Mr. Sinhā, the able and ingenious lawyer, has been enacting the drama of love with the civil surgeon's ugly daughter Miss Kāmat because he needs Mr. Kāmat's help in one of his suits. But more serious thoughts arise in Mr. Sinhā's mind. It would not be a bad idea to marry Miss Kāmat if the surgeon paid a handsome dowry, say twenty to twenty-five thousand rupees. After all, one does not sell oneself to a girl by marrying her! The subjudge's daughter Tibbī is a young thing, still in her teens and a first-year student at college. Her servant Ghuré has been with the family since she was an infant and is old enough to be her grandfather. But she shouts at him and boxes his ears because he is a bit tardy in obeying her commands. The old man retires to his shack and sheds tears of sorrow at his sad lot. For Tibbī he is nothing more than a hired hand, and she has every right to insult and clobber him. There is no bond above and beyond the cash nexus.

Prem Chand's chief concern in the novel is, however, with the bond that links the author to his public. We have it on the testimony of his eldest son, Mr. Shripat Rāi, that *Mangal-Sutra* was designed to be an autobiographical work like *Godān*. "[Prem Chand] wanted to demonstrate on the basis of his own sense of values that craftiness is not indispensable for success . . . to show that an honest, industrious, and straightforward man could win the type of success which should be the envy of other people, and that this world is not irrevocably opposed to well-earned distinction."[12] It is not quite clear in what sense Mr. Shripat Rāi regards *Godān* as an autobiographical work, but the comment is helpful to an understanding of *Mangal-Sutra*. Dev Kumār, in succumbing to the line of thinking that his life had not been a success because he had failed to amass a large fortune, accepts the values of a commercial civilization represented by his own son and Mr. Sinhā. Prem Chand was often assailed by doubts about his own success in life but he was intelligent enough to recognize that he would be repudiating his own principles if he measured success in terms of money. Criticism of Dev Kumār's conduct is thus an act of self-assurance and rededication on his part, imparting to the novel a testamentary value and a unique poignancy and depth beyond anything he ever wrote.

But if the onslaught of commercialism is one danger to the sanity of modern man, an equally serious one is that of intellectualism when it is divorced from moral and spiritual considerations. It is not reason but faith which holds society together. The prevalence of injustice in the world, of the vicious flourishing and the virtuous floundering, is enough to make us doubt the existence of a moral order and find shelter in a kind of nihilism. Acceptance of nihilism will, however, destroy the very foundations of society and will be an invitation to chaos. The abstract reasoning by which Dev Kumār rationalizes his own greed is one of the greatest snares to which thinking minds are susceptible. This slide into a sort of opportunistic cynicism is a self-violation, a betrayal of everything he had held sacred in life, a cowardly surrender to the spirit of the age.

Mangal-Sutra is a deeply disturbing, even frightening, work, and affords a glimpse into Prem Chand's mind during the last days of his life. The world he portrays is one of moral and spiritual decay, a world in which the most sacred bonds which have united man to man with hoops of steel are being snapped as if they were gossamer threads. The literary artist is in his eyes no mere peddler of wares: he is the salt of the earth, a prophet and a sage, a friend, philosopher, and guide, who is linked to his public by an auspicious bond. When persons like Dev Kumār lose their moorings, it is a real cause for concern. Sādhu Kumār's presence in the novel indicates that there is some ground for hope, but the prospect is grim enough nonetheless.

CHAPTER 8

The Short Stories

RĀMVILĀS Sharmā expressed the view that if a choice were to be made for a permanent place in literature between Prem Chand the novelist and Prem Chand the short-story writer it would definitely be in favor of Prem Chand the novelist. Indranāth Madān, on the contrary, believes that undoubtedly great though Prem Chand is as a novelist, he is even greater as a short-story writer, and Gangā Prasād Vimal agrees with him.[1] A comparison of this sort is, I think, hardly proper, for Prem Chand the short-story writer and Prem Chand the novelist are not different persons. Moreover, on the basis of the stories alone, Prem Chand would not have attained the status he has as a literary artist. The imaginative power and the creative talent needed to produce novels like *Rangabhumi* and *Godān* and for writing a short story are not of the same order. The stories are not stunning as technical achievements either. A majority of them are of indifferent quality, some being outrightly bad. His work as a novelist is therefore central to his achievement. But the more than 250 short stories make the Prem Chand World richer and fuller.[2] They constitute an authentic and impressive portrayal of Indian life, political, social, and cultural, particularly in his native Uttar Pradesh in the first third of the present century. They were an important and effective means of maintaining contact with his expanding reading public, for they commanded an audience larger even than the novels. Pouring out in a steady stream in the leading Hindi and Urdu periodicals of the day, they kept him in the public gaze and increased his popularity. They made him responsive to his public, making him select stories for the magazines with an eye on their character and clientele.

The most striking thing about Prem Chand the story writer is his unusually wide range. He writes about Rājās and Nawābs, aristocrats and gentlemen from country squires to highly Westernized and newfangled Sāhibs; middle-class men from shabby-genteel clerks and shopkeepers to professional people like doctors, lawyers, judges, professors, and engineers. The whole spectrum of village life is home ground to Prem Chand, and he has a sensitive and unerring eye for the fine gradations of social structure based on rank and status, caste and class, age and sex, which characterize the complex Indian society. Women have his love, and respect, and he vents his anger against the social conventions which sanction and perpetuate their inferior status, just as he condemns political and social exploitation, moral and religious corruption.

It is difficult to trace any definite development in Prem Chand's art as a story writer. He was capable of writing a superb tale like *Baré-Ghar-kī-Bétī* (The Daughter of a Noble Family, 1910, VII, xi) at the beginning of his literary career and equally capable of writing a bad one like *Khudāi-Fozdār* (God's Policemen, 1934, II, ii) toward the end.[3] The good stories, instead of belonging to a distinct period, stand out as high points in an expanse of work of average quality. If a principle of classification must be sought, it is more likely to be found in ideological predilections. For instance, in stories written during the earliest phase, roughly from 1907 to 1918, the past is almost always praised and idealized. Quite a few of these stories are romantic tales, full of exaggerated sentiments and sensational and melodramatic incidents, written in a rhetorical style. The society they reveal is medieval and feudal, following the traditions of chivalry and courtly love. In "The Most Priceless Object in the World," Prem Chand's first story, the beloved, who is a Persian princess, a paragon of beauty and intelligence, tells her lover that she will accept him only if he brings to her the most priceless object in the world. The lover sets out in search of this object and, after three attempts, succeeds in bringing from the fabled land of Hindusthān the last drop of blood shed by a young warrior who had died fighting for his country. The princess is pleased and accepts him. There is considerable change in the atmosphere, tone, and manner of the stories written during the next ten years. New themes are introduced in stories like "The Daughter of a Noble Family," *Béti-Kā-Dhan* (The Daughter's Money, 1915, VIII, iii) and *Panch Parméshwar* (The Voice of God, 1916, VII, xii), but the attitudes and values are essentially the same. As in the historical tales representing the Bundelās' or the Rājputs' valor and sense of honor which we have already discussed in chapter 4, Prem Chand glorifies ancient Indian ideals and traditions. Even in stories which deal with contemporary life he seems to be uneasily poised between realism and nostalgia.

A distinct change in themes and outlook is noticeable around 1920 when, under Gandhi's influence, he resigns his position in government. *Mrityu-ké-Peeché* (After Death, 1920, VI, vii) is a comparative evaluation of two life styles, one solely dedicated to self-advancement, another to a cause, and looks like the justification of the fateful step he had just taken, a self-vindication. An author-journalist wants to serve his society and his country, but his wife would rather have him make money by becoming a lawyer. The wife experiences a change of heart when the journalist is idolized and worshipped by the public after his death. This Gandhian concept of change of heart also dominates *Pashu-sé-Manushya* (From Animal to Man, 1920, VII, xi). Man is intrinsically good; he becomes degraded by poverty, exploitation, and tyranny, but his humanity can be restored through kindly treatment and a noble example. Gandhi's influence can also be seen in Prem Chand's efforts to promote understanding between Hindus and Muslims through stories like *Hazrat Alī* (The Apostle Ali, 1923), *Nabī-kā-Neeti-Nirvāha* (The Prophet's Adherence to Justice, 1924, *G. D.*, II, xvii), *Kshamā* (Pardon, 1924, III, xx), and *Mandir-aur-Masjid* (The Temple and the Mosque, 1925, *G. D.*, II, xviii). Political stories like *Rajya-Bhakta* (Faithful Servant of the State, 1923, VI, xviii) and *Shatranj-ké Khilārī* (The Chess-Players, 1924, III, xxvii) are indicative of his changed attitude toward the past. Instead of treating it as a source of inspiration, he exposes the decadence and corruption of Indian society in the eighteenth and nineteenth centuries under rulers like the Nawābs of Oudh, which made India fall like an overripe fruit in the foreigners' lap. To the corruption of the rulers was added the ravenousness of the higher orders which made them exploit the lower ones and plunge them into a benumbing poverty. This is really the point of one of Prem Chand's best stories, *Qafan* (The Coffin-Cloth, 1936), in which two *chamārs*, father and son, callously while away their time while the son's wife is dying of severe labor pains. They collect money to pay for her coffin-cloth but squander it all away on drink. In *Savā-Sér-Géhun* (A Seer-and-Quarter of Wheat, 1924, IV, xv), almost a first sketch for *Godān*, we get a glimpse of the vicious system of usury through which higher-caste moneylenders entrap guileless and unsuspecting peasants into a situation of eternal serfdom. In *Doodh-kā-Dām* (Payment for Milk, 1934, II, xvi) a *harijan* woman, neglecting her own son, brings up an upper-caste child by breast-feeding. When she and her husband die, her orphan child is severely punished because he is caught playing with his upper-caste "brother." This is how the high-caste family pays him for his mother's milk. *Sadgati* (Salvation, 1931, IV, ii) is the story of a *chamār* who is exploited by a Brahmin to the extent that he dies of hunger and thirst. In *Mandir* (The Temple, 1927, I, xxiii) an untouchable woman is kicked out and her child killed when she tries to enter the temple to pray for recovery of the sick child. In *Thākur-kā-Kuān* (The Squire's Well, 1932, I, ix) an untouchable dies of drinking putrid water because the higher castes would not allow his wife to get clean water from their well.

Prem Chand's burning desire to revitalize his nation impels him to write stories uncovering evils which were the bane of Hindu society—unequal marriages in *Nayā-Vivāha* (New Marriage, 1928, II, xxv); marriages arranged by parents against the wishes of young men and women who are to be married in *Vidrohī* (The Rebel, 1928, II, viii); the despicable system of dowry which makes even honest people succumb to the temptation of bribes to marry off their daughters in *Sajjantā-kā-Dand* (Punishment for Decency, 1916, VIII, xviii); the incredible injustices of Hindu laws of inheritance under which the widow has no right to the property of her dead husband in *Bĕton-wālī-Vidhvā* (The Widow With Sons, 1932, I, iv); the tragic consequences of ill-treating girls who have become widows and of banning the remarriage of child widows in *Dhikkār* (Shame, n.d., I, xvi). Prem Chand's continued concern for fallen women comes out in stories like *Veshyā* (The Prostitute, 1923, II, iii) in which he restates his belief that it is corrupt societies rather than individuals who are mainly responsible for the prevalence of the tragic evil of prostitution. Many of these women would relinquish their lives of sin and suffering if only courageous men were to come forward and marry them. Prem Chand has no patience with persons like Dayā Krishna in the story who choose to enact the drama of love but whose courage fails when the moment of decision arrives. In *Sevā-Sadan* he had raised the tough question of what was to be done with the children of prostitutes, particularly the daughters: who would marry them? *Aagā-Peechā* (The Implications, 1928, IV, x) and *Do Kabrĕn* (Two Graves, 1930, IV, iv) depict the sad lot of these unfortunate creatures who, for no fault of their own, have to suffer the scorn of society. In the first, a prostitute's daughter and a *chamār* youth, both bright students in college, fall in love with each other, but the young man suffers a loss of nerve as the day of marriage approaches. In the second a liberal-minded professor marries a prostitute's daughter, but when she is spurned by his social circle, he begins ill-treating her. The proud girl commits suicide.

In 1929 - 30 when the freedom movement had again entered an active phase and there was widespread civil disobedience in the country in response to the Mahātmā's call, Prem Chand wrote about a dozen stories which are notable for their patriotic fervor—*Mā* (Mother, 1929, I, iii), *Patnī-sé-Pati* (From Wife to Husband, 1930, VII, ii), *Sharāb-kī-Dukān* (The Tavern, 1930, VII, iii), *Juloos* (The Procession, 1930, VII, iv), *Samar-Yātrā* (Journey to the Battlefield, 1930, VII, vi), *Maikoo* (1930 VII, v), *Jail* (1931, VII, i), and *Tāwān* (Fine, 1931, I, xxiii). His outlook in these stories is stern and uncompromising. He satirizes the Indians' fondness for tall talk but lack of capacity for action, and he has no use for men who compromise with tyranny and injustice and plead their helplessness in the name of wife and children. A man must do whatever is right and essential for the health and growth of his own soul without fear of incurring anybody's displeasure. Cowardice and pusillanimity are unforgivable sins. And it is interesting that in almost each of these stories the women are more courageous and high-principled than the men, acting as their conscience and instigating them to act rightly. "From Wife to Husband" shows a nationalistic wife and a toadyish husband, who is ashamed of being an Indian and apes English ways. When he is insulted and abused by his British officer for his wife's donation of money to the Congress, he wakes up and resigns his position, accepting the leadership of his wife. "The Procession" too projects woman in the same role.

Interesting and fairly good sometimes though these stories are, they read more like tracts, containing long passages of political and social propaganda. His best stories are those in which he can keep his ideological and moral enthusiasm in check and furnish vignettes of social life in the village or the home as in *Ālgyojhā* (Splitting, 1929, I, xxiv), *Subhāgī* (1930, I, ii), *Pus-kī-Rāt* (The Winter Night, 1930, I, ii), *Ghar-Jamāi* (The Resident Son-in-Law, 1929, I, x); or present studies of human nature as in *Atmā Rām* (1920, VII, ix), *Boorī-Kākī* (The Old Aunt, 1921, VIII, xiv), *Mukti-Mārg* (The Way to Salvation, 1924, III, xxv), *Sujān Bhagat* (1927, V, xxiv), *Pisan-Hārī-Kā-Kuān* (The Miller-Woman's Well, 1928, V, xv), *Swāminī* (The Mistress, 1931, I, viii), *Idgāh* (The Place for the Celebration of Id, 1933, I, ii), *Lottery* (1935, II, xxiii), and *Qafan* (The Coffin-Cloth, 1936). Equally attractive are other tales written in a lighter vein, some based on experiences of childhood and school days, *Chorī* (Theft, 1925, V, ix), *Kazākī* (1926, V, xi), and *Gullī-Dandā* (1929, I, xii). They derive their charm from the author's narrative skill, his manipulation of tone which enables him to establish rapport with the reader through taking him into confidence. He is ironic and witty, the master of a simple, lucid, and flowing style, which is a beautiful blend of Hindi and Urdu and the very model of conversational Hindusthānī. His humor can range from the subtle and ironic—*Baré-Bhāi Sāhib* (The Elder Brother, 1934, I, v), *Muft-kā-Yash* (Unmerited Credit, 1934, II, xiv)—to the boisterous and hilarious as in *Motor-ké-Cheenté* (The Spattering from the Car, n.d., II, v), *Aakhirī-Heelā* (The Last Pretext, 1931, I, xxii), *Demonstration* (1931, IV, vi), *Rasik-Sampādak* (The Amorous Editor, 1933, I, xxvi), and the stories featuring Moté Rām Shāshtri—*Satyāgraha* (1923, III, xxix) and *Moté Rāmjī Shāshtrī* (1928, *G. D.*, II, xxii). He can combine devastating satire with mordant humour as in *Boram* (The Crazy One, 1923, VII, xxii). In a world where an utter lack of principle is synonymous with worldly wisdom, the man who has conscience and acts from principle is bound to be considered crazy.

Many of these stories are excellent, but I will select here for closer analysis two which I consider to be superb—*Boorī-Kākī* (The Old Aunt) and *Shatranj-ké-Khilārī* (The Chess-Players). "The Old Aunt" is the story of an old woman whose one craving is for food. "Old age," Prem Chand observes, "is the last stage of covetousness, when all the desires are concentrated at one point. For the Old Aunt this point was the palate" (VIII, 160). Many years ago she had given all her property to her nephew, Pandit Buddhi Rām, with whom and whose wife, Rupā, she is now residing. Though the property yields a comfortable income, the Aunt is never given enough food to satisfy her hunger. Once there is a big feast because the Pandit's son is going to be married. The Old Aunt is enchanted by the beautiful aroma of the food that is cooking in the house and is waiting to be invited to share it. Hours pass but no invitation is forthcoming; the old woman, unable to restrain herself any longer, crawls out of her dark hole and shows up by the place where the food is cooking. Rupā, beside herself with anger, pounces on the Old Aunt "as a frog pounces on an earthworm" and abuses her roundly. The Aunt crawls back to her hole. All the guests have had their dinner and even the meanest servants have eaten, but no food has been offered to the Old Aunt as a punishment for her indiscretion. Thinking that all the guests must have left by now, she crawls once again out of her hole, but, alas, some guests are still eating. This time her nephew Pandit Buddhi Rām sees her and it is his turn to fly into a rage. He bodily lifts the old woman, carries her to her hovel, and drops her like a sack of potatoes. The Old Aunt's transgressions were by now beyond the limits of forgiveness because her frequent appearances were likely to create the impression that her nephew and his wife were starving her. It is now eleven in the night and everyone in the house is sleeping soundly. The only exception is Buddhi Rām's youngest daughter, Lādli, who is attached to the old woman and resents her parent's ill treatment of her. She has saved her own share of the food and, now making sure that everyone is fast asleep, she takes it to the Old Aunt. The Aunt eats the food which, instead of allaying her appetite, only aggravates it. She asks Lādli to take her to the place where the guests had eaten. The child, unable to guess the aunt's intentions, obeys her and takes her to the place where lay the leftovers from the guests' plates. The poor, hungry, witless woman begins swallowing the pieces of fried bread. Just at this moment Rupā wakes up. She sees the Old Aunt, a Brahmin, eating the rejected food, is stunned at the incredible sight and struck with the fear that the wrath of the gods might descend on her and her family. She lifts both her hands to the Almighty and prays for His mercy. She then lights the lamp, puts every kind of food available in a big plate and places it before the Old Aunt. "Like a simple child who forgets all about beatings and insults as soon as she gets some sweets," the old woman is having a hearty meal and is showering blessings on Rupā and her family from the innermost recesses of her soul.

"The Old Aunt" is a simple but powerful story, illustrating Prem Chand's profound insight into human nature, the elemental force of passions and appetites in man. The social setting is real and convincing, the cruelties of family life, the morbid fear of public opinion and of the anger of the gods having been graphically portrayed. Rupā would have no mercy on the old woman who had given her entire property to herself and her husband, but when she realizes her responsibility for the degradation to which she has pushed the old woman, the fear of nemesis unnerves her.

"The Chess-Players" is a historical tale, a tale of the nineteenth century when the British as an imperial power were steadily extending their sway over India. It draws a picture of the decadent society of the North Indian state of Oudh, under the rule of the notorious Wājid Ali Shāh, when Lucknow, the capital city, was sunk in sensuality and no one of importance had the slightest concern with what was going on in the rest of the world.

Mirzā Sajjad Alī and Mīr Roshan Alī, two wealthy noblemen who have *jāgirs* with a rental income of thousands of rupees a year, are representative of the ruling elite. Chess is a passion with them. Every morning after breakfast both friends sit down to play the game, and once it is begun they forget everything else in the world. Calls for dinner and other important engagements are just ignored. The game used to be played at the Mirzā's house, but there comes a stage when his wife refuses to put up with it any longer. The noble players transfer its venue to the Mīr's house. The latter's wife had welcomed the Mīr's absence because it had allowed her liberty to carry on her own affairs. Now the continuous presence of her husband around the house becomes a nuisance, and she thinks of a stratagem to scare him away. At her instance, one of her lovers comes disguised as an officer bringing a summons to military service from the Nawāb. The chess players have absolutely no inclination to honor obligations of this nature. To avoid further embarrassment once again they shift the venue of their game, this time to an old dilapidated mosque outside the city, across the river Gomatī. About ten o'clock one fine morning, when they are deeply absorbed in their game, they see the East India Company's forces marching in the direction of the capital city. These are British forces moving in to occupy the capital and topple the Nawāb's government. The chess players see the army, assess its size and the nature of its armament—about five thousand troops with heavy guns—but still remain engrossed in their game. About four in the afternoon the troops are returning:

> Nawāb Wājid Alī Shāh had been taken prisoner, and the army was taking him to an unknown destination. In the city there had not been either any activity or any killing. Not a drop of blood had been shed. Never before had the independent ruler of a nation been defeated so peacefully, without any bloodshed whatsoever. This was not a manifestation of the kind of non-violence which pleases the gods. It was the cowardice which provokes tears even in the most cowardly. The Nawāb of the vast kingdom of Oudh was being taken away as a prisoner, but Lucknow was entranced in the sleep of sensuality. This was the limit of political decadence. (III, 277)

The Mīr is winning the games today and has, therefore, no thoughts to spare for the fate of the Nawāb or of the state. But the Mirzā, who is losing, does regret the Nawāb's fall. This is taken by the other as an excuse to divert attention from the game, and he starts using harsh words against the Mirzā. It leads to an altercation. Both of them, aristocrats as they are, wear arms: they fight like two knights, for "though they were voluptuaries, they were no cowards." They had become devoid of all political sense and did not understand why they should have laid down their lives for their king or country. But the same people who did not shed a single tear for their king died fighting for the make-believe Vizier in the game of chess.

"The Chess-Players" has all the marks of a great story and illustrates Prem Chand's art at its best. It shows his skill in creating a historical atmosphere: the diction, idiom, modulation of voice in which the characters speak single them out as courtiers of the highly civilized Kingdom of Oudh. The narrative flows smoothly and there is unity of effect coming from the artistic combination of incident and tone. What Poe said of Hawthorne's stories can be applied to Prem Chand's with equal truth: "Every word *tells*, and there is not a word which does not *tell*. . . ." The game of chess becomes symbolic of the nobles' divorce from reality and escape into the world of make-believe. Life itself is a game for them, devoid of any seriousness or sense of purpose.

Prem Chand has written some of the most delightful stories featuring animals. Occasionally they have a political import but the author is tactful enough to keep his propagandistic impulse under control. *Svatva-Rakshā* (Defense of Dignity, 1922, VIII, xix) is the story of a self-respecting horse who in spite of a savage beating refuses to sacrifice his dignity by working on a Sunday. He could respond to love but would neither be bought up nor coerced into submission. *Do-Bailon-kī-Kathā* (The Story of Two Bullocks, 1931, II, xii) is a masterly fable describing how two intelligent and spirited bullocks foil the schemes of their oppressors. The story opens with the suggestion that perhaps too much decency is not suited to this world.

> Don't you see how shabbily Indians are being treated in [South] Africa; why they are not allowed to enter the United States? The poor fellows don't drink, save something for the rainy day, work awfully hard, do not quarrel with anybody, remain patient even in the face of provocation. Still they have acquired a bad name. It is said that they lower the standard of life. Had they learnt to pay back in the same coin, they would have been called civilized. The example of Japan is before us. One victory was enough to get her an honourable place among the civilized nations of the world. (II, 149)

The narrator's fraternal solidarity with the bullocks as victims of oppression and his admiration for their spirit of independence shine like a gold thread throughout the fable.

Prem Chand's 265 stories, in which he rarely repeats himself, are a massive body of work, standing as living evidence of his fertile imagination and marvelous powers of invention. They constitute one of the most ambitious delineations of life ever attempted by a creative writer. But their technique is striking for its simplicity. Many of them have roots in the long and rich Indian tradition, oral and written—jokes, proverbs, parables, fables, anecdotes, folktales; myths and legends from the epics and the *Purānās;* and Persian and Arabic tales of love, intrigue, and adventure. Prem Chand was aware of the work of modern Western short-story writers like Balzac, Maupassant, Chekhov, Tolstoy, Dostoevski, and Gorki and occasionally experimented with new techniques. His real admiration, however, was reserved for the old masterpieces—the *Mahābhārata,* the *Upanishads,* the *Buddha-Jātaks,* and the Bible—for their pure imagination, original execution, and splendor of style *(Aims of Literature,* 40). Among the moderns, too, he likes best storytellers such as Tolstoy, "some of whose stories are of the same calibre as the parables of old" *(Aims,* 42 - 43). It is not surprising therefore that his own stories follow the same technique. They are, first, good yarns in which events follow their normal chronological order, characters are described as well as dramatically revealed through action and dialogue and have a representative quality which invests their destinies with a significance larger than their own. But there are certain newer elements too. "The best story," Prem Chand observes, "is one which is based on some psychological truth" *(Aims,* 51), and there are quite a few of his own which have a plot of interior action. The real charm of his stories, however, lies in their naturalness and simplicity, in the very absence in them of the expedients and contrivances which are characteristic of conscious art.

CHAPTER 9

Conclusion

OF the various critical evaluations of Prem Chand's creative achievement Nagendra's is perhaps the most challenging.[1] He feels that Prem Chand is not in the first rank of creative artists. Nagendra admires Prem Chand's natural, profound, and pervasive humanism, emphasizes the documentary value of his work, and doubts whether there is another Hindi writer who presents such a comprehensive picture of the sociopolitical, economic, and communal life during the first three phases of the Gandhian era. But he sees explicit limits to Prem Chand's genius. His outlook is practical or utilitarian in the best sense of the word: he has no interest in truth or beauty for their own sake. Humanism is after all a materialistic philosophy: Prem Chand could only assimilate Gandhi's reformism but was unable to appreciate the spiritual side of Gandhism. He is not a creative writer of the first rank because his critical gaze is concentrated on contemporary problems; he has touched but rarely or not at all the perennial questions of life. There is a lack of intellectual solidity and firmness in him, qualities which can come only from deep philosophical thinking. Normality—the distinctive trait of Prem Chand's personality, according to Nagendra—can attain only the second rank; to be first-rate one must be exceptional.

Nagendra illustrates the sharp stratification of the reading public in our time between what may, for the sake of convenience, be called the high-brow and the middle-brow. To the high-brow critic Prem Chand is moralistic, didactic, reticent on the intimate aspects of life, earnest but blind to the possibilities of art and to the complexities of human nature. Ilā Chandra Joshī,[2] for instance, regards his characters, particularly the female ones, as some sort of embodied abstractions, lacking in individuality and vitality.[2] Prem Chand was a child of his age, and he has the strengths and weaknesses of his position. It is not simply that he is not interested in technical experimentation for its own sake or betrays a strange naiveté in matters of pure art: he would have considered preoccupation with concerns of this nature irrelevant and even irresponsible, as is clearly seen in his disapproval of the romantic school of Urdu poetry. Art for him is, unquestionably, the servant of life, and he would have answered his Art-for-Art's-sake critics with Samuel Butler's well-known sally: "Who is art that it should have a sake?" His best novels are, at bottom, the creation of a profoundly moral impulse. This does not mean that he did not have enough respect for the real, for fidelity to the surface as well as the depth of experience. Though he cannot match George Eliot's intellectual and analytical power, Dostoevski's piercing insight into the innermost recesses of the human soul, and Tolstoy's wide experience of the world, he has most of these qualities in ample measure to make him a writer of considerable stature. He has a rich and robust creative talent, a depth of understanding, insight, and moral passion to identify himself with a broad spectrum of humanity, specially the humble and the weak. He has the born creative artist's ability to render life in concrete detail, the sage's moral fervor to inspire and enthuse men to love decency and goodness. Though a master of humor and sarcasm, he is not a mere entertainer or chronicler of the social scene. He is really in the line of reformers and sages like Rām Mohan Roy, Vivekānand, and Tagore who strove to regenerate the Indian nation by arousing it from its millenial slumber. In the manner of the Victorian sages, the thinkers like Emerson, Thoreau, and Whitman, he points to his countrymen the dangers of an unthinking infatuation with modern materialism and reminds them of the moral and spiritual values enshrined in their own culture. In many of his earlier novels he seems to be retreating from the full and gloomy consequences of his own vision and taking refuge in a sentimental utopianism. Man's life is, however, based on faith and hope: Prem Chand's utopian dreams are merely a manifestation of his strong faith in man. He was doing the same thing which *philosophes* like Condorcet and Godwin, Romantic poets like Blake and Shelley, and sages like Gandhi with his utopian ideal of *Rāma Rājya* ("The Reign of Rama") have done—using his creative imagination to project the vision of a perfect society in which men, transcending their selfishness and greed and forgetting the distinctions of caste and creed, could live like brothers and sisters. This does not mean that he is an armchair philosopher or an idle dreamer. Poverty and want were living realities to him because he was nurtured in their midst and had experienced them himself. But his faith in man led him to strive ceaselessly to impress on his upper-class countrymen the criminality of the economic and social system which they upheld. The degree of success attained by him is difficult to measure; maybe even scores of Prem Chands would not succeed in disturbing the self-serving slumber of the classes. But he did bring into existence the Hindi-Urdu social-political novel, molding the attitudes of younger writers who acknowledged their indebtedness to him and some of whom chose to call themselves "progressive." He helped widen the meaning of literature from the belletristic conception of Urdu writers and even those of the Bhārtendu school in Hindi. Literature for him implied a vigorous involvement with ideas and issues, rather than an escapist withdrawal into the realms of fantasy and romantic love. He evolved a style which is simple, lucid, sinewy, and supple, a finely tempered instrument which can with equal ease capture the raciness and vigor of the villager's idiom and the urbanity and elegance of that of the Persianized elite. Dr. Rāmvilās Sharmā is right to emphasize the magnitude of his achievement in this regard.[3] And the list of contributors to *Prem Chand Smriti* (1959) gives us some idea of the impact he has made on the world of letters in Hindi and Urdu.

The recurrent figure in Prem Chand's novels is the idealistic young man who is called upon to choose between his own self-advancement and the claims of the community and the nation. Some of these young men turn out to be lifeless and wooden like the "virtuous" heroes of even great novelists like Scott, George Eliot, and Tolstoy. Thus we have Amrit Rāi, Pratāp Chandra, Vinaya Singh, Prem Shankar, and Shankhdhar. But there are others who are living and real—Balrāj, Chakradhar, Amarkānt. So are heroes of another sort—Surdās and Horī—and the whole cast of other characters who enliven the novels in which they appear—Gyān Shankar, Totā Rām, Munshī Vajradhar, Lālā Samarkānt, Devīdīn, Gobar, Mātā Dīn. It is grossly unfair to describe, as Ilā Chandra Joshī does, the creator of Suman, Nirmalā, Manoramā, Jālpā, and Dhaniā as a painter of abstractions who had no understanding of women. They do not cease to be vital just because they symbolize something. Each of them is, in Henry James's terms, "a strikingly figured symbol," because each is also "a thoroughly pictured character." Moreover, stature as a writer cannot be assessed in isolation from the nature and amount of the output. Emily Brontë wrote one novel, but Dickens created a world. Prem Chand composed some outstanding works which are masterpieces in their own right—stories like *Boorī Kākī*, *Qafan*, and *Shatranj-kê-Khilāri;* novels like *Sevā-Sadan, Rangabhumi* and *Godān*. But to form a true estimate of his genius it is necessary to consider the totality of his output, which constitutes one of the most varied, rich, and comprehensive renderings of life ever achieved by a writer of fiction. The Prem Chand World in its richness and variety invites comparison with the Scott, Dickens, Hardy, and, with certain limitations, even the Tolstoy World.

Prem Chand was keenly aware of the indifferent status of the creative writer in Indian society. There was not likely to be much confusion about his place if he had composed works of piety and learning: if he were a Brahmin like Tulsīdās he would have been honored and revered, if a low-caste man like Kabīr he would have been unworldly and unconcerned about social status. The position would have been clear too if he were independently wealthy like Bhārtendu Harish Chandra and Tagore, or held an official position like Bankim Chandra. But if he did not belong to any of these categories, there was no option for him but to seek the patronage of the rich and powerful and adopt the servile attitude of the supplicant. Prem Chand is one of the first Indian writers who refused to follow this path, who was fiercely independent in his attitude and absolutely uncompromising in his principles. His resignation from government service was in its own way a step as momentous as Tagore's renunciation of the knighthood in 1919, his letter to the Mahārājā of Alwar as significant as Dr. Johnson's famous letter to Lord Chesterfield.[4] How courageous these actions were can be realized when we compare Prem Chand with figures such as Sir Mohammad Iqbāl, who, with all their genius, could not resist the temptation of following the path of opportunism and alliance with the powers that were.

Thus great as Prem Chand is as a novelist, short-story writer, essayist, and moralist, he is equally great as a humanist, a humanitarian, and a man. An estimate of his worth as a creative writer which ignores his distinction as a human being runs the risk of being partial and inadequate.

Notes and References

Chapter One

1. See Prem Chand, "*Jeevan-Sār*—Life in Essence," in *Mangal-Sutra and Other Works* (Allahabad, n.d.), p. 351.

2. See Madan Gopāl, *Munshī Prem Chand: A Literary Biography* (Bombay and New York, 1964), p. 72.

3. Hence the title of the biography written by his son Amrit Rāi, *The Soldier with the Pen* (Allahabad, 1962). Henceforth referred to as *Life*.

4. *Gupt Dhan* (Allahabad, 1962), p. 9.

5. *Mangal-Sutra,* p. 351.

6. Shivrānī Devī Prem Chand, *Prem Chand: In the Home* (Delhi, 1956), p. 264.

7. Madan Gopāl, *Prem Chand: Labourer with the Pen* (Delhi, 1965), p. 54. This book in Hindi should be distinguished from Madan Gopāl's other book *Munshī Prem Chand: A Literary Biography* (Bombay & New York, 1964) which is written in English.

8. See Prem Chand's letter to Tāj in which he says: "Gandhi is due here to-day (February 8, 1921)." *Chitthī-Patrī* (Allahabad, 1962), II, 129. Shivrānī Devī errs in saying that Gandhi visited Gorakhpur in 1920. See *In the Home*, p. 47.

Chapter Two

1. Shivrānī Devī Prem Chand, *In the Home*, p. 264

2. Jainéndra Kumār, *Prem Chand: His Creative Personality* (Delhi, 1973), p. 60.

3. Ibid., p. 63

4. Ibid., p. 65.

5. Jainéndra, p. 57; Rāmvilās Sharmā, *Prem Chand and his Age* (Delhi, 1967), p. 191.

6. "Rahbar," *Prem Chand: Life, Art and Creative Work* (Delhi, 1962), p. 294.

7. See his *Prem Chand: Man and Literary Artist* (Allahabad, 1961), pp. 473 - 75.

8. See Krishna Chandra Pāndey, *Ruling Elements in Prem Chand's Philosophy of Life* (Allahabad, 1970), pp. 187 - 89.

9. See his letter to Nigam, 6 March 1913, requesting the latter to pay the subscription on his behalf. *Chitthī-Patrī*, I, 19.

10. See Madan Gopāl, *Labourer with the Pen* (Delhi, 1965), p. 70; also Mahesh Prasād's essay in *In Memory of Prem Chand,* ed. Amrit Rāi (Allahabad, 1959), pp. 162 - 65.

11. *Kuch Vichār* (Allahabad, 1973), p. 71.
12. See his comment to Shivrānī Devī in her *Prem Chand: In the Home,* p. 97.
13. *Labourer,* p. 70.
14. *Ruling Elements,* pp. 200 - 201.
15. Sophia's comments in *Rangabhumi* (Allahabad, 1973), p. 38 are worth noting.
16. Jainéndra Kumār's testimony on this point is the most authoritative. See also Prem Chand's letter to him in his *Prem Chand,* p. 39.
17. "Shri Krishna and the Future World," in *Vividh Prasang* (Allahabad, 1962), III, 141.
18. Introductory note on George Eliot to his Hindi adaptation of *Silas Marner* as *Sukhdās* (Allahabad, 1972), p. 6.
19. "Vivekānand," in *Kalam, Talwār aur Tyāg* (Allahabad, 1972), I, 106.
20. "Gopāl Kirshna Gokhalé," ibid., II, 41.
21. This novel was published in 1907. Anti-British feeling was pronounced after the partition of Bengal in 1905. It is, therefore, likely that the novel was written earlier. For the date of composition see Amrit Rāi's introductory remarks in *Mangalācharan* (Allahabad, 1962).
22. See Bhabāni Sen Gupta, *Communism in Indian Politics* (New York, 1972), p. 11.
23. See Sir Isaiah Berlin, *Karl Marx: His Life and Environment* (London, 1963), p. 7.
24. *In Memory of Prem Chand,* p. 258. For the date of publication of this essay see Amrit Rāi's Preface.
25. See his *Prem Chand,* p. 71.
26. Alfred G. Meyer, *Communism* (New York, 1960), p. 12.
27. Shivrānī Prem Chand, *In the Home,* p. 95, and "Great Sacrifice," in *Vividh Prasang,* II, 437 - 42.
28. See "Rahbar," p. 271.
29. *Prem Chand,* pp. 71 - 72.
30. See Jawāharlāl Nehru, *Autobiography* (London, 1936), pp. 365 - 66.
31. For all these see Bhabāni Sen Gupta, p. 422.
32. See Sir Isaiah Berlin's brilliant essay *The Hedgehog and the Fox: an Essay on Tolstoy's View of History* (New York, 1953), p. 8.
33. Ibid., p. 69.
34. Berlin, *Karl Marx,* p. 6.

Chapter Three

1. See Kamal Kishore Goyankā, *Prem Chand's Craftsmanship* (Delhi, 1973), Appendix I, pp. 543 - 44.
2. See *The Great Tradition* (London, Penguin Books, 1962), p. 10.
3. See "The Aim of Literature," in *Sāhitya-kā-Uddéshya* (Allahabad, 1967), pp. 10 - 13.
4. Rāmvilās Sharmā, *Prem Chand,* pp. 30 - 31.

5. Nalin Vilochan Sharmā, *The Hindi Novel, Especially Prem Chand* (Patnā, 1968), p. 6.
6. See the essay "Life in Essence," in *Mangal-Sutra*, p. 350.
7. For all these see "Sharar and Sarshār," in *Vividh Prasang*, I, 59 - 72.
8. See Goyankā, *Prem Chand's Craftsmanship*, Appendix II, p. 545.
9. The characterization is Nehru's in *The Discovery of India* (New York, 1946), p. 356.
10. For an admirable and scholarly analysis see Goyankā, pp. 522 - 27.
11. See the essay "Old Times: New Times," published in *Zamānā* of February 1919; reprod. *Vividh Prasang*, I, 258 - 69.
12. For an able exposition of this Grand Design see Nehru, *Discovery of India*, pp. 328 - 32.
13. See B. N. Pāndey, *The Break-up of British India* (London & New York, 1969), p. 117 n.
14. See the rough outline of the novel in Madan Gopāl, *Labourer*, pp. 169 - 70.
15. For the controversy about its date of composition see Goyankā, pp. 68 - 70.

Chapter Four

1. See Amrit Rāi's Preface to *Mangalācharan*, p. 9.
2. For the point that the Hindi version is a rendering and not a translation see Goyankā, p. 87. Goyankā, however, seems to be mistaken about its date of publication. He thinks that it was published in 1907, the date which the Hindi rendering bears; but, as Amrit Rāi points out, the Hindi rendering which bears the date 1907 is the second edition, not the first, as Goyankā thinks. The first edition bears no date. See Rāi's Preface to *Mangalācharan*, pp. 7 - 8; Goyankā, pp. 56 - 57.
3. In the letter to Nigam, quoted by Rāi, ibid., p. 7.
4. S. A. Wolpert, *Tilak and Gokhalé* (Berkeley, 1962), p. 297; quoted by Pāndey, *British India*, p. 50.
5. See his letter to Nigam in which he informs him about his learning to write in Hindi because there was no scope in Urdu: "Which Hindu has earned distinction as a writer in Urdu that should encourage me to think that I shall also do so?" *Chitthī-Patrī*, I, 46.
6. Ibid., p. 13. Amrit Rāi regards Prem Chand's "Hindu-ism" as merely a whim. I differ from him. See *Life*, p. 153.
7. See *Labourer with the Pen*, p. 44 n.
8. See, for instance, the couplet in *Mangalācharan*, p. 365.
9. See "Rahbar," p. 166; Amrit Rāi, *Life*, p. 119. For Kamar Rais's opinion see Goyankā, p. 58.
10. "I have been born in the line of Gāndhārī [the wife of Dhritrāshtra, the father of the Kauravas in the *Mahābhārata*, who kept her eyes covered because her husband was blind] and Savitrī [the woman who through the power of her devotion to her husband pleased Yamarāja, the god of death,

and persuaded him to restore her husband to life]." See *Vardān* (Delhi, 1968), p. 157.

11. See Prem Chand's preface to the first edition of the novel in Goyankā, p. 122.

12. See Goyankā, pp. 60 - 61; Amrit Rāi, *Life*, p. 654.

13. Madan Gopāl, *Labourer*, p. 110.

14. *Prem Chand and his Age*, p. 32.

15. "Rahbar's" assessment is perhaps an extreme example but not entirely untypical. He characterizes him as an unprincipled opportunist. See *Prem Chand*, p. 176.

16. See Manmath Nāth Gupta, *Prem Chand*, pp. 168 - 69. He refers to the criticism of Rām Ratan Bhatnāgar.

Chapter Five

1. Goyankā, pp. 62, 64.

2. Madān, while recognizing the influence of capitalism which upholds unrestrained individualism, sees hardly any difference between capitalism and liberalism. Madān's entire analysis emphasizes the social aspect of the novel. See his *Prem Chand: An Analysis*, rev. ed. (Delhi, 1968), pp. 52 - 63.

3. See his *Prem Chand and his Age*. pp. 44 - 58. Hazārī Prasād Dwivedī also sees the iniquity of the *zamindāri* system as the main theme of the novel. See Madān, ed. *Prem Chand: Thought and Art* (Benaras, n.d.), p. 38.

4. Joan Bennett quoted by Walter Allen, *The English Novel* (London, 1957), p. 211.

5. The phrase is C. B. MacPherson's. See his *The Political Theory of Possessive Individualism: Hobbes to Locke* (Oxford, 1962).

6. Haribhāu Upādhāya quoted by Manmath Nāth Gupta in his essay on *Rangabhumi* in *The Genius of Prem Chand*, ed. Indranāth Madān (Allahabad, 1967), p. 63.

7. Ibid., p. 70.

8. Ibid., p. 67.

9. Sharmā, *Prem Chand and his Age*, p. 170.

10. "Mahātmā Gandhi does not want revolution; neither has revolution brought about the redemption of any country." *Vividh Prasang*, II, 78. This seems to be categorical.

11. Sharmā, p. 79.

12. See M. N. Gupta's essay in Madān's collection, p. 67.

13. See the essay "The Benefits of Swarāj," in *Vividh Prasang*, II, 270. The essay is a very clear exposition of Prem Chand's views on economic problems.

14. See the essay "Shri Krishna and the Future World," in *Vividh Prasang*, I, 140 - 43.

15. Goyankā makes the interesting suggestion that Prem Chand produced *Rangabhumi* as a modern version of Tulsidās's Rāmāyana in response to

Mahātmā Gandhi's demand on Hindi writers. See *Prem Chand's Craftsmanship*, p. 271.

16. For Dostoevski's compliment to Dickens on the creation of Pickwick see his letter to his niece Sofiya Ivanova in Steven Marcus, *Dickens: From Pickwick to Dombey* (New York, 1965).

17. See Prem Chand's letter to Nigam dated 17 July 1926, *Chitthi-Patrī*, I, 162; also Goyankā, pp. 66 - 67.

18. See Madan Gopāl, *Literary Biography*, p. 230. The English is Prem Chand's own.

19. See B. N. Pāndey, *British India*, pp. 121 - 22.

20. The distinction was made by Tolkien in his lecture at the University of St. Andrews in 1938, the year he was beginning work on *The Lord of the Rings*. A revised version of the lecture is printed in *Tree and Leaf* (London, Unwin Books, 1964).

21. See the stimulating discussion of this problem in Malcolm Bradbury, *Possibilities: Essays on the State of the Novel* (London; Oxford Paperbacks, 1973).

22. See Pāndey, *British India*, p. 117 n., quoted above in chapter 3, II.

23. *Literary Biography*, p. 230.

24. For all these see *Chitthī-Patrī*, I, 143, 149, 157.

Chapter Six

1. *Literary Biography*, p. 251
2. *Prem Chand and his Age*, p. 65.
3. *Prem Chand's Craftsmanship*, p. 312.
4. *Prem Chand and his Age*, p. 64.
5. *Prem Chand's Craftsmanship*, pp. 344 - 46.
6. Ibid., p. 545.
7. See Amrit Rāi, *Life*, pp. 399 ff.
8. *Literary Biography*, p. 274.
9. *Life*, pp. 445 - 46.
10. For details about the Meerut Case see Bhabāni Sen Gupta, *Communism in Indian Politics*, p. 11.
11. *Prem Chand's Craftsmanship*, pp. 372 - 73.
12. "Materialism is the soul of Western civilization." *Vividh Prasang*, I, 174.
13. *Prem Chand's Craftsmanship*, p. 374.
14. See *Chitthī-Patrī*, I, 178 - 79.

Chapter Seven

1. For the controversy regarding its date of composition see Goyankā, pp. 70 - 72.
2. *Prem Chand and his Age*, p. 85.
3. Goyankā, p. 417.
4. For the political background see Pāndey, *British India*, pp. 130 - 34;

for Prem Chand's views see the essays "Long Live Congress," "The Present State of the Nation," and "Gandhi's Victorious March," in *Vividh Prasang*, II, 72 - 83.

5. See Goyankā, pp. 72 - 73. Madan Gopāl, in *Literary Biography*, p. 427, takes March 1935 as the date of the novel's completion, but Goyankā draws attention to Prem Chand's letter to B. C. Roy of Faridpur (Bengal) in which he said that he was still working on the novel. *Chitthī-Patrī*, II, 264. This shows that it must have been completed either in Dec. 1935 or Jan. 1936.

6. Sharmā, *Prem Chand and his Age*, p. 101; Rāmdīn Gupt, "Disillusionment with Gandhism" in Indranāth Madān, *Prem Chand: Evaluations and Evaluations* (Allahabad, 1971), p. 72; Goyankā, pp. 485, 448.

7. See *Vividh Prasang*, II, 471.

8. See Gupt's essay in Madān, *Evaluations*, p. 76.

9. Goyankā, p. 455. For irrelevance of the world of the town see Jainéndra Kumār, "Prem Chand's *Godān:* Had I Written it," in *Prem Chand: Creative Personality*, p. 166.

10. The degrading effect of poverty is also the theme of the story *Qafan*, published in 1936.

11. See *Mangal-Sutra and Other Works*, ed. Amrit Rāi, p. 389.

12. See Shripat Rāi's letter to M. N. Gupta in the latter's *Prem Chand*, p. 357.

Chapter Eight

1. See Rāmvilās Sharmā, p. 114; Madān, *Prem Chand: An Analysis*, 4th ed. (Delhi, 1968), p. 112; Gangā Prasād Vimal, *Prem Chand* (Delhi, 1968), p. 81.

2. The exact number of stories written by Prem Chand is difficult to determine. The total number included in the eight volumes of *Mānsarovar* and the two of *Gupt Dhan* is 259. Amrit Rāi's list in *Life* contains 225. There are about 40 stories which appear in the two collections mentioned above but which do not feature in Rāi's list. The total number should thus be close to 265. If Rāi's guess that about thirty to forty stories more should still be found is correct, the total number would exceed 300, surely a formidable body of work. See Rāi's Preface to *Gupt Dhan*.

3. References are to *Mānsarovar*, 8 vols. and *Gupt Dhan* 2 vols. The year of publication of the story is mentioned first, followed, in large Roman numerals, by the number of the volume in which it was published, then its number within the volume itself in small Roman numerals. References to *Gupt Dhan* are singled out by the use of the abbreviation *G. D.*

Chapter Nine

1. See his "Prem Chand: A Comprehensive Examination," in *The Genius of Prem Chand*, ed. Indranāth Madān (Allahabad, 1967), pp. 9 - 18.

2. See his "Personality and Art," ibid., p. 27.
3. See *Prem Chand and his Age*, p. 151.
4. Madan Gopāl relates how he spurned the U. P. Governor's offer of the title "Rāi Sāhib" in 1927; see *Literary Biography*, p. 259.

Selected Bibliography

PRIMARY SOURCES

This bibliography makes no claim to exhaustiveness. The main emphasis is on Prem Chand's works and only a few of the most important biographical and critical studies are listed. After mentioning the dates of first publication, I have listed the editions to which reference has been made in the text.

1. Novels

Asrār-é-Mābid (Mystery of the House of God). Serialized in *Āvāz-é-Khalk*, 1903; *Premā*. Allahabad: Indian Press, 1907; *Roothi-Rāni* (The Estranged Queen). Serialized in *Zamānā*, 1907. All these reprinted in *Mangalācharan: Prem Chand ké Ārambhik Upannyās* (The Invocation: Prem Chand's Early Novels) Comp. and ed. by Amrit Rāi. Allahabad: Hans Prakāshan, 1962.

Kishnā. Pub. in Urdu, 1907. Text not available.

Vardān (Benediction). Bombay: Granth Bhandār, 1920; rpt. Delhi: Govindrām Hāsānand, 1968. (Hindi version of *Jalvā-é-Isār* pub. in 1912).

Sevā-Sadan (The Abode of Service). Calcutta: Hindi Pustak Agency, 1918; rpt. Allahabad: Saraswati Press, 1973.

Premāshram (The Abode of Love). Calcutta: Hindi Pustak Agency, 1922; rpt. Allahabad: Saraswati Press, n.d.

Rangabhumi (The Stage). Lucknow: Gangā Pustak Mālā, 1925; rpt. Allahabad: Saraswati Press, 1973.

Kāyākalp (Metamorphosis). Benaras: Saraswati Press, 1926; rpt. Allahabad: Saraswati Press, 1971.

Nirmalā. Serialized in *Chānd*, 1925 - 26; rpt. Allahabad: Saraswati Press, n.d.

Pratigyā (The Vow). Serialized in *Chānd*, 1927; rpt. Allahabad: Hans Prakāshan, 1971.

Ghaban (Embezzlement). Benaras: Saraswati Press, 1931; rpt. Allahabad: Hans Prakāshan, 1971.

Karmabhumi (The Arena). Benaras: Saraswati Press, 1932; rpt. Allahabad: Hans Prakāshan, 1973.

Godān (The Giving of the Cow). Benaras: Saraswati Press, 1936; rpt. Allahabad: Saraswati Press, 1972.

Mangal-Sutra va Anya Rachnayén (The Auspicious Bond and Other Works). 1948; rpt. Allahabad: Saraswati Press, n.d.

2. Short Stories

Mānsarovar. 8 vols. Allahabad: Saraswati Press, 1966 - 71.

Gupt Dhan (Hidden Treasure). Edited by Amrit Rāi. 2 vols. Allahabad: Hans Prakāshan, 1962.

3. Letters and Essays

Chitthi-Patri (Letters). Compiled and edited by Madan Gopal and Amrit Rāi. 2 vols. Allahabad: Hans Prakāshan, 1962. The most reliable of all source books on the chronology of Prem Chand's life and books besides being a storehouse of information on other matters.

Vividh Prasang (Miscellaneous Thoughts). Compiled and edited by Amrit Rāi. 3 vols. Allahabad: Hans Prakāshan, 1962. Contributions to *Zamānā, Hans, Jāgaran,* and other writings. Most valuable.

Kuch Vichār (Some Thoughts). Allahabad: Saraswati Press, 1973. Essays on the language problem and on literature.

Sahitya-kā-Uddeshya (The Aim of Literature). Allahabad: Hans Prakāshan, 1967. Essays on literature in general and on individual authors.

4. Plays and Books for Children

Sangrām: Ek Sāmājik Nātak (Conflict: A Social Play). Calcutta: Hindi Pustak Agency, 1923; rpt. Allahabad: Saraswati Press, 1967.

Karbalā. Lucknow: Gangā Pustak Mālā, 1924.

Mahātmā Sheikh Sa'di. Gorakhpur: Hindi Pustak Agency, 1918.

Bā Kamālon ké Darshan. Allahabad: Rāmnarain Lāl, 1928; rpt. later as *Kalam, Talwār aur Tyāg* (The Pen, the Sword and Sacrifice). Allahabad: Saraswati Press, 1973. Biographical sketches of eminent men.

Rām Charchā (Talking about Rām). Lahore: Lājpat Rāi & Sons, n.d.; 8th ed. Allahabad: Hans Prakāshan, 1969.

Durgā Dās. 9th ed. Allahabad: Hans Prakāshan, 1969.

5. Translations

Prem Prabhākar. n.d. About 20 stories of Tolstoy presented in an Indian setting.

Shab-é-Tār (The Dark Night). Serialized in *Zamānā*, 1919. Urdu translation of Maurice Maeterlinck's *Sightless*.

Ashk-é-Nadāmat (Tears of Shame). Pub. in *Kahakashān*, Lahore, 1920. Urdu trans. of Dickens' *The Story of Richard Doubledick*.

Sukhdās. 1923; rpt. Allahabad: Saraswati Press, 1972. A condensed Hindi version of George Eliot's *Silas Marner*.

Ahankār (Pride). Calcutta: Burrā Bazar Kumār Sabhā, 1923; rpt. Allahabad: Hans Prakāshan, 1970. Hindi trans. of Anatole France's *Thais*.

Āzād-Kathā (The Story of Āzad). 2 vols. 1925 - 26. 6th ed. 1 vol. Allahabad: Saraswati Press, 1972. Hindi trans. of Sarshār's *Fasān-é-Āzād*.

Chāndī-kī-Dibiā, Nyāya, Hartāl. 1934. Trans. of Galsworthy's *Silver Box, Justice,* and *Strife* for the Hindusthāni Academy. Not certain whether these were published. Also translated some portions of Nehru's *Glimpses of World History.* Publication uncertain.

6. Translations of Prem Chand's Own Work in English

The Giving of the Cow. A translation of *Godān* by Gordon C. Roadarmel. Bloomington: Indiana University Press, 1968.

The Chess Players and Other Stories. Ten stories translated by Gurdial Mallik. Orient Paperbacks, Delhi: Hind Pocket Books, 1967.

The World of Prem Chand. Selected Stories translated by David Rubin. Bloomington: Indiana University Press, 1969.

SECONDARY SOURCES

1. Books on Prem Chand

GOYANKĀ, KAMAL KISHORE. *Prem Chand ké Upannyāson kā Shilp Vidhān* (Prem Chand's Craftsmanship in his Novels). Delhi & Allahabad: Saraswati Press, 1973. A highly intelligent and exhaustive consideration of the novels by a leading Prem Chand scholar. Most reliable from the scholarly point of view.

GOPĀL, MADAN. *Kalam kā Mazdoor* (Laborer with the Pen). Delhi: Rājkamal Prakāshan, 1965. Biography in Hindi by one of the greatest authorities on Prem Chand. A mine of information.

______. *Munshi Prem Chand: A Literary Biography.* Bombay & New York: Asia Publishing House, 1964. The only full-length biography in English; indispensable.

GUPTA, MANMATH NĀTH. *Prem Chand: Vyakti aur Sahityakār* (Prem Chand: Man and Literary Artist). Allahabad: Saraswati Press, 1961. A Marxist interpretation of Prem Chand's work; original and stimulating at times but also tendentious and misleading.

GURU, RĀJESHWAR. *Prem Chand: Ek Adhyayan* (Prem Chand: A Study). An excellent discussion of Prem Chand's sociopolitical views.

KOTHĀRI, KOMAL AND DETHĀ, VIJAYADĀN., eds. *Prem Chand ké Pātra* (Prem Chand's Characters). Delhi: Akshar Prakāshan, 1970. Perceptive analysis of the characters in the novels.

KUMĀR, JAINENDRA. *Prem Chand: Ek Kriti Vyaktitva* (Prem Chand: His Creative Personality). Delhi: Purvodaya Prakāshan, 1973. A fascinating analysis of Prem Chand's personality by one of his closest friends and admirers who is an eminent novelist himself; also contains some important letters. A thoughtful and profound study.

MADĀN, INDRANĀTH. *Prem Chand: El Vivéchan* (Prem Chand: An Analysis). Delhi: Rajkamal Prakāshan, 1950; rpt. 1968. A sociopolitical examination of the novels and stories. Interesting and enlightening.

______, ed. *Prem Chand: Chintan aur Kalā* (Prem Chand: Thought and Art) Benaras: Saraswati Press, n.d. Essays on the novels and stories by various hands. Valuable.

———, ed. *Prem Chand Pratibhā* (Prem Chand's Genius). Allahabad: Saraswati Press, 1967. Collection of essays on novels and stories. Valuable.

———, ed. *Godān: Mulyānkan aur Mulyānkan* (Godān: Evaluations and Evaluations). Allahabad: Neelābh Prakāshan, 1971. Useful.

PĀNDEY, KRISHNA CHANDRA. *Prem Chand ké Jeevan Darshan ké Vidhāyak Tatva* (Ruling Elements in Prem Chand's Philosophy of Life). Allahabad: Rachnā Prakāshan, 1970. A useful study of Prem Chand's social, political and religious thought.

PRASĀD, SAROJ. *Prem Chand ké Upannyāson mén Samsāmayik Paristithion kā Pratiphalan* (Presentation of Contemporary Problems in Prem Chand's Novels). Allahabad: Rachnā Prakāshan, 1972. A typical thesis turned into a book; a useful introduction to the social and political conditions in India.

PREM CHAND, SHIVRĀNI DEVI. *Prem Chand: Ghar Mén* (Prem Chand: In the Home). Delhi: Ātma Rām & Sons, 1956. Fascinating memoirs of Prem Chand by his wife giving an intimate account of his domestic life. An indispensable source book.

PURI, RAKSHĀ. *Prem Chand Sāhitya Mén Vyakti aur Samāj* (The Individual and Society in Prem Chand's Literary Work) Delhi: Ātma Rām & Sons, 1970. Another typical thesis turned into book.

"RAHBAR," HANSRĀJ. *Prem Chand: Jeevan, Kalā aur Krititva* (Prem Chand: Life, Art and Creative Work). 2nd ed. Delhi: Ātma Rām & Sons, 1962. Useful in some ways but unreliable from the scholarly point of view.

RAI, AMRIT, ED. *Prem Chand Smriti* (In Memory of Prem Chand). Allahabad: Hans Prakashan, 1959. A most valuable collection of essays by Hindi and Urdu scholars who had known Prem Chand personally. Also contains the texts of *Mahajani Sabhyata* and *Mangal-Sutra*.

———. *Prem Chand: Kalam ka Sipahi* (Prem Chand: The Soldier with the Pen). Allahabad: Hans Prakāshan, 1962. Prem Chand's biography by his able son. One of the best biographies in Hindi, written in vigorous, lucid, and scintillating prose. Rai's imagination gives it sometimes the feel of a novel. An indispensable source book. An appendix for the first time provides an authentic list of the short stories and fixes their chronology.

SHARMÁ, NALIN VILOCHAN. *Hindi Upannyās: Vishéshtaha Prem Chand* (The Hindi Novel; especially Prem Chand). Patnā: Gyānpeeth Private Limited, 1968. A most valuable study of the tradition of the Hindi novel and Prem Chand's place in it.

SHARMĀ, RĀMVILĀS. *Prem Chand aur Unkā Yug* (Prem Chand and his Age). rev. ed. Delhi: Rājkamal Prakāshan, 1967. A brilliant and incisive examination of Prem Chand's fiction from the socioeconomic point of view by an eminent scholar and perhaps the most distinguished of his critics.

SINGH, BHARAT. *Prem Chand ké Nāri Pātra* (Prem Chand's Female Characters). Delhi: Pustak Prachār, 1973. Another thesis-book.

VIMAL, GANGĀ PRASĀD. *Prem Chand*. Delhi: Rājkamal Prakāshan, 1968. A perceptive and scholarly evaluation of Prem Chand's fiction.

2. General, including Books on Indian History and Culture

ALLEN, WALTER. *The English Novel: A Short Critical History*. London: Phoenix House Ltd., 1954.

BERLIN, SIR ISIAH. *The Hedgehog and the Fox: An Essay on Tolstoy's View of History*. New York: Simon & Schuster, 1953.

______. *Karl Marx: His Life and Environment*. 3rd ed. London and New York: Oxford University Press, 1963.

BONDURANT, JOAN. *Conquest of Violence: The Gandhian Philosophy of Conflict*. Berkeley: University of California Press, 1961.

BRADBURY, MALCOLM. *Possibilities: Essays on the State of the Novel*. London and New York: Oxford University Press, 1973.

BRECHER, MICHAEL. *Nehru: A Political Biography*. Boston: Beacon Press, 1962.

BROOMFIELD, J. H. *Elite Conflict in a Plural Society: Twentieth-Century Bengal*. Berkeley: University of California Press, 1968.

CHANDRA, BIPAN. *The Rise and Growth of Economic Nationalism in India*. New Delhi: People's Publishing House, 1966.

CHAUDHURI, NIRAD C. *The Autobiography of an Unknown Indian*. Berkeley: University of California Press, 1968.

de BARY, WILLIAM THEODORE, ed. *Sources of Indian Tradition*. New York: Columbia University Press, 1958.

EMBREE, AINSLEE T. *India's Search for National Identity*. New York: Knopf, 1972.

FISCHER, LOUIS. *The Life of Mahatma Gandhi*. New York: Collier Books, 1962.

GANDHI, MOHANDAS K. *An Autobiography: The Story of My Experiments with Truth*. Boston: Beacon Press, 1964.

HEIMSATH, CHARLES H. *Indian Nationalism and Hindu Social Reform*. Princeton: Princeton University Press, 1964.

IONS, VERONICA. *Indian Mythology*. London: Paul Hamlyn, 1968.

ISAACS, HAROLD. *India's Ex-Untouchables*. New York: John Day, 1964.

KRIPALANI, KRISHNA. *Rabindranath Tagore: A Biography*. London: Oxford University Press, 1962.

LEAVIS, F. R. *The Great Tradition*. London: Penguin Books, 1962.

LEWIS, MARTIN D., ed. *Gandhi: Maker of Modern India?* Boston: D.C. Heath & Co., 1965.

LOW, D. A., ed. *Soundings in Modern South Asian History*. Berkeley: University of California Press, 1968.

MACPHERSON, C. B. *The Political Theory of Possessive Individualism: Hobbes to Locke*. Oxford: Clarendon Press, 1962.

MAJUMDAR, R. C. *History of the Freedom Movement in India*. 3 vols. Calcutta: Firma K. L. Mukhopadhayay, n. d.

MASON, PHILIP. *India and Ceylon: Unity and Diversity.* London: Oxford University Press, 1967.

MARCUS, STEVEN. *Dickens: From Pickwick to Dombey.* New York: Basic Books, 1965.

McCULLY, BRUCE TIEBOUT. *English Education and the Origins of Indian Nationalism.* Gloucester, Mass.: Peter Smith, 1966.

MEYER, ALFRED G. *Communism.* rev. & enl ed, New York: Random House, 1963.

MOON, SIR PENDEREL. *Gandhi and Modern India.* New York: Norton, 1969.

MUJEEB, M. *The Indian Muslims.* Montreal: McGill University Press, 1967.

NEHRU, JAWAHARLAL. *An Autobiography; with Musings on Recent Events in India.* London: John Lane, 1936.

———. *The Discovery of India.* New York: John Day Company, 1946.

OVERSTREET, GENE D. and WINDMILLER, MARSHALL. *Communism in India.* Berkeley: University of California Press, 1960.

PANDEY, B. N. *The Break-up of British India.* London: Macmillan; New York: St. Martin's Press, 1969.

SEAL, ANIL. *The Emergence of Indian Nationalism: Competition and Collaboration in the Later Nineteenth Century.* Cambridge: Cambridge University Press, 1968.

SEN GUPTA, BHABANI. *Communism in Indian Politics.* New York: Columbia University Press, 1972.

SRINIVAS, M. N. *Social Change in Modern India.* Berkeley: University of California Press, 1967.

TOLKIEN, J. R. R. *Tree and Leaf.* London: Unwin Books, 1964; Boston: Houghton Mifflin, 1965.

WOLPERT, STANLEY R. *Tilak and Gokhale: Revolution and Reform in the Making of Modern India.* Berkeley: University of California Press, 1962.

———. *A New History of India.* New York: Oxford University Press, 1977.

Index